shown.

How to create
the Perfect
RIDING
HORSE

Perry Wood

David and Charles

A DAVID & CHARLES BOOK
Copyright © David & Charles Limited 2007

David & Charles is an F+W Publications Inc. company
4700 East Galbraith Road
Cincinnati, OH 45236

First published in the UK in 2007

Text copyright © Perry Wood 2007

Perry Wood has asserted his right to be identified as author
of this work in accordance with the Copyright, Designs and
Patents Act, 1988.

A catalogue record for this book is available from the British
Library.

ISBN-13: 978-0-7153-2693-0 hardback
ISBN-10: 0-7153-2693-7 hardback

ISBN-13: 978-0-7153-2914-6 paperback
ISBN-10: 0-7153-2914-6 paperback

Printed in China by Shenzhen Donnelley Printing Co., Ltd
for David & Charles
Brunel House   Newton Abbot   Devon

Commissioning Editor Jane Trollope
Assistant Editor Emily Rae
Designer Jodie Lystor
Production Controller Beverley Richardson
Photographer Bob Atkins

Visit our website at **www.davidandcharles.co.uk**

David & Charles books are available from all good bookshops;
alternatively you can contact our Orderline on 0870 9908222
or write to us at FREEPOST EX2 110, D&C Direct, Newton
Abbot, TQ12 4ZZ (no stamp required UK only); US customers
call 800-289-0963 and Canadian customers call 800-840-5220.

Contents

Introduction

Many years ago, I ran a riding vacation business in the South West of England, which meant we were constantly on the lookout for good horses to buy. Sellers and horse dealers would often ask the question *'What are you looking for exactly?'* and we would jokingly reply *'The perfect riding horse!'* I say 'jokingly', because we didn't believe the perfect riding horse existed: but that was then. After many more years working with horses I have changed my mind and now believe it *is* possible to create the perfect riding horse: one that is perfect for your own wishes and requirements...

WHAT IS YOUR IDEA OF THE PERFECT RIDING HORSE?

Every horse is unique and so is every rider, which means that everyone's idea of what makes the 'perfect riding horse' is likely to be different, too. For some, the perfect horse would be a slow, steady, solid type, whereas others may crave the excitement of a spirited, prancing hot-blood... the list is likely to be as varied as the people reading this book.

This book is about creating the perfect riding horse for YOU, and it will give you the tools, tips, techniques and suggestions you need to create your own perfect riding horse. By 'perfect' I don't necessarily mean there is no room for improvement or no more challenges left to overcome: in fact, some people's idea of the perfect riding horse might be one that is always challenging!

MY IDEA OF THE PERFECT RIDING HORSE

My idea of the perfect riding horse is a horse who enjoys being ridden as much as I enjoy riding him. I want the horse to want to work *with* me and accept my role as leader, which means achieving what I want without force, punishment or domination. I want the horse to be a good friend and partner, but I also want him to be a spirited, athletic, responsive and supple performer, to take things in his stride and enjoy the odd challenge himself... not much then! Provided you follow a simple, step-by-step, intelligent and objective approach, I believe it is possible to create a fantastic riding horse from most horses.

Much of the riding in this book is based on the principles of classical riding or classical dressage. Classical riding is the foundation for most forms of riding we see in the world

today and was developed for purely practical reasons. It is the distillation of 2,500 years of riding and is the systematic training of the horse to be light, responsive, courageous and athletic. The original classically trained horse would have been used in warfare or, as he still is today in Iberia, in the bullring. So the training had real purpose and application, and the bottom line was that your life might depend on how well you trained your horse!

I think you will see, as you work your way through this book, that the perfect riding horse is a genuine all-rounder whose 'dressage' training is not confined to the riding arena, but that his training opens up a whole world of possibilities, as he becomes more and more of a joy to ride and to be with.

Of course, to create the perfect riding horse you could say we have to be the perfect rider! That's why I have included tips and 'perfect rider' boxes throughout the book; pointers that will help you to help your horse be the best he

can be – and you may be pleasantly surprised, because he will probably turn out better than you ever thought possible.

NOTE: Throughout this book I have used the terms 'he' or 'his' when referring to horses. This is as a matter of clarity and does not reflect any other agenda. The horses I am working with in the book are of both sexes.
NOTE II: I use the word 'training' in this book to describe the various ways we can work to improve the way the horse responds. You could equally use 'educate', but to me 'training' is the best choice of word because we are developing the horse's physique as well as teaching him things.

I asked some of my students to describe the qualities they would like in their perfect riding horse. Here's what they said:

• Lightness
• Spirited
• Great partner
• Forward-thinking
• Would go through fire for me
• Sensitive
• Manoeuvrable – dancing partner
• Responsive to my aids
• Sensible
• Listens and focuses on me
• Best friend
• Self-confident
• Trusting
• Curious

Choosing the Right Horse

It is possible to spend a lot of time and money in pursuit of the 'perfect horse', but it doesn't always pay off – even the greatest looking, 'well bred' horses can fall short of the mark.

More important than the amount of money and time spent 'up front', is the amount of commitment and time invested afterwards. The way I see it, there are three key ingredients for the perfect riding horse: conformation, temperament and time. As long as a horse has a reasonable conformation and a nice temperament, I believe that with time and training it is possible to create a wonderful riding horse from almost any horse.

Generally speaking, the better his conformation and balance, the more potential a horse has, and the quicker and easier your progress should be. If he is physically well made for the job you want, he will find it easier to do what you ask of him, too.

Although conformation is important, temperament can be even more so. When a horse is willing to work with you and is open to learning and trying things, it becomes a lot easier to further his training and get the kind of results you want. Aside from which, it isn't a lot of fun riding a horse who is unhappy in his work, however marvellous his conformation. For me, the joy comes from sharing the journey and experiences with an equine partner who enjoys the riding as much as I do. I want his full spirit to shine through and yet still have him following my directions.

Conformation and temperament are certainly key ingredients, but what makes the ultimate difference is what you actually do with the horse and how much time you put in. You could have the best made, kindest tempered horse in the world, but if you don't train him or do very much with him, he still won't become a great riding horse. You may not consider yourself to be a horse trainer, but in reality, every time you sit on a horse you are training it, either to go better or to go worse!

CONFORMATION AND MOVEMENT

Conformation is a very subjective thing; everyone has a different idea of what looks good to them. The most important thing is to have a horse who is built for the job and has the right type of movement for what you want him to do.

It is important to be able to see your horse moving at liberty in all three paces – walk, trot and canter – in order to have an idea about his natural movement and what he is capable of… or what he needs help with.

The key is to look at how your horse is made, as this will affect how he works and how you will need to work with him. Here are some pointers to help you:

• **The neck** The horse uses his neck as an important balancing tool, so a neck which is a nice length (not too short or too long) with good muscle development along the top is useful. A neck which is too short and/or too deep can make the horse less easy to guide, and possibly strong on the reins. An overly long, thin neck can make it hard to collect the horse or guide him. The angle the neck comes up out of the wither also influences the kind of ride you will get: a neck set on too low may make the horse feel low in front and put him on his forehand a lot. A neck set on too high can make it difficult for the horse to round through his back and collect. Horses with a very high neck are often quite tense and highly strung.

• **The back** A horse with a long back can be difficult to collect and more prone to having soreness in the back. Horses with a dipped back tend to have a weakness at the place where they need to bear the weight of the rider, making it harder to collect them or to have them going softly.

Fantastique has quite a long back, but she steps well underneath herself with her hind legs and carries her front end nicely. She has a naturally arched overall shape, and is free in both her shoulders and her forelegs.

You can see from this picture that even though Arnie has started to raise his neck, he is naturally built with more weight on his forehand than his hindquarters. This can make it difficult for him to really 'open up' in his movement and be light and forward-going. Despite this, he is a very powerful horse with a lot of potential.

• **The hind legs** In order to perform well in any sphere, even as a nice comfy trail-riding horse, he needs to have good flexibility in the joints of his hind legs. Hind legs that are stiff or do not bend well, particularly at the hocks, can make it difficult for the horse to perform well in any sphere. It is also important to make sure the horse's hind legs move in a precisely even rhythm. If the rhythm between the two legs is even slightly broken, it implies a weakness in one of them. When you look really closely, many horses seem to be slightly uneven in the rhythm of their legs, but assuming it is not too marked, it is something we can work on as the horse becomes stronger and more supple.

• **Forelegs and shoulders** Some horses have plenty of movement in the hindquarters but the shoulders and forelegs don't really swing, so the flow of energy coming up from the back of the horse gets somehow blocked at the front. The horse needs freedom in the shoulders to move well throughout his frame. As with the hind legs, it is important that the forelegs move in a precisely even rhythm.

• **Overall carriage** For the horse to be easy to ride and work with, it is beneficial for him to have good natural carriage, which means he has an overall look of going 'uphill' from the back to the front and has a rounded or arched shape throughout his whole frame (when he is looked at from the side).

• **Overall balance** Imagine a set of scales, with the wither as the centre, and look for balance between the forehand and hindquarters. If the scales are tipped to the front (horse has too much front) or to the back (horse has too much back end), it can make it difficult for the horse to find his natural balance. Add the weight of a rider to the equation and it is probably not going to be the easiest partnership.
NOTE: People sometimes look at a young horse who is croup high (back is higher than the front) and say it's just the way he is growing and his front will catch up… but this is not always the case.

• **Build** 'Horses for courses' is a very well known phrase, and although it may seem obvious, it is so important to have a horse built for the job he is required to do. Lighter horses have the benefit of speed and quickness of turning, but heavier horses have the benefit of more power and sheer physical strength.

Arnie may not be perfectly physically balanced, but he has a good attitude.

TEMPERAMENT

As we have said, a good temperament can be more important than the physical build of the horse… if he has a good attitude it may be easier to get him to be how you want than if he is physically perfect but impossible to deal with. Arnie may not be perfectly physically balanced, but he has a good attitude and is interested in working with me, which means we can enjoy riding together, make good progress and get some great results. Of course being a cold-blooded, heavier type of horse it can sometimes require me to approach him with tact and patience to get a good tune out of him.

LOOKING OBJECTIVELY AT YOUR HORSE

Look objectively at the horse you are working with now, not to judge him and what he does as being 'good' or 'bad', but to really see what equine material you are working with. An honest and unemotional review can help you to see what areas need addressing for improvement. Look at how he moves, how he is built, what his neck is like, how reactive, quick or sluggish he is. Which is his stiff side? Which is his easy side? Which canter lead does he favour? What does he enjoy, and what worries him? How responsive is he to each of the aids: reins, legs and seat? Your answers will give you clues about what you most need to work on.

Arnie is a Lippizaner X Shire: quite a heavily built horse.

THE HORSES IN THIS BOOK

The two horses featured in this book are quite different from each other, and have very different histories. One is a heavier, slower type, and the other is a finer, sharper and more reactive type, making them both very different to work with.

Arnie is a former trekking horse. He is a 12-year-old Lipizzaner X Shire. He is very laid back, and not always full of energy or forwardness. I have been working with him about three or four days a week for the last 18 months. As you

can see, he is quite a heavy build, with a strong neck. Arnie's weight is naturally on his forehand and his head carriage is quite low. With all this in mind, I have to create energy in him, have him lighten his forehand, and make sure he stays light and soft in his mouth. He is also prone to be inattentive, so I have to keep his mind on the job by keeping a conversation going (see 'Listens to the Rider', page 36).

With this heavier type of horse it can be a challenge to ask them to move with lightness: to be light on their feet and responsive to the aids.

Fantastique is light on her feet and very sensitive.

Fantastique is 13 years old and has Lipizzaner, Fell pony and Lusitano in her. I have been riding her consistently for about eight years. She is very quick, sensitive, reactive, intelligent and athletic, which could all add up to her being quite challenging – and so she has been, on the odd occasion. Fantastique's neck is set quite high and she is quick to lighten her forehand (levade is always available should it be requested!), but that doesn't always help me to round her back, because she can also rush. With all this in mind, I have worked with her to build and maintain a trusting relationship, so I can calmly channel all her talents, energy and attributes, rather than struggle against them. I have also worked on asking her to lower her neck and settle into a regular rhythm, rather than rush. With her quick mind, it has been important to regularly give her new experiences and challenges, in order to give her something to think about.

Perry's Tip

Most of us don't start with perfect equine material to work with, but that doesn't mean you can't work with the horse you have in order to create something perfect for you.

✓ DOs
- Have a really objective look at the horse you are working with: notice how he is made and how he moves, and see how this is reflected in what he is like to ride and work with.
- Take time, and more time… think of it as a journey without an end… a piece of living sculpture that is never quite finished (if it were, you might get bored quite quickly!).
- Remember it is always on-going work to maintain the horse in peak performance condition.
- Notice what you do with the horse on days when he goes really well… and do more of it, more often.

✗ DON'Ts
- Don't think you can make a steeplechaser out of a Shire horse!
- Don't work with a horse that is too much for you – it could be the perfect horse for someone else.
- Don't think it is a quick or easy job to make a perfect riding horse.
- Don't compare you and your horse's progress to anyone else… every horse and rider develops at a different rate.

Because of her confirmation and lightness, a movement such as levade is quite easy for Fantastique. This level of athleticism may not be everyone's 'cup of tea', but to me it is wonderful when properly channelled.

Good to Handle

Advertisements in the newspaper offering riding horses for sale often say something like 'Good to catch, shoe, box and clip', which is one way of saying a horse is 'good to handle'.

However, I also like a horse to be good to lead, groom, mount and tack up, as well as being generally nice to be around. There are many books and experts these days concentrating on handling issues with horses, which is a big subject in itself, but as this is a book about creating the perfect riding horse, I want to concentrate on some of the things that affect us directly when we ride. It is sometimes the case that a horse is great to handle and difficult to ride, or vice versa; but more often than not, a horse who is well mannered, attentive and accepts your boundaries when handled, displays the same qualities when ridden.

LEADING

Leading is incredibly important because it sets the basis for your communication with the horse, even before you consider mounting him. If a horse is attentive, soft on the rope, stops and walks on just to your body language, walks at your speed and stays respectfully out of your space (not crowding you) when being led, he will probably be all of those things under saddle, which is exactly how we want him to be. Leading is a really good way to tell what the horse is going to be like to ride: whether he is going to be overly keen, lazy, braced in his neck and mouth, easily distracted, attentive to your aids or not, and so on.

Leading is a great place to start to establish YOU as the leader and the horse as the follower, and from there you can build a rewarding and successful partnership. Let us be quite clear about this leadership issue: horses weigh about half a ton, and they are very strong and fast compared to us – so although we may dream of having an equal partnership with the horse, it is naturally going to be a partnership of unequals.

Because horses often mirror how they are to ride in how they lead, we can do quite a lot to establish responsiveness by working on teaching them to be great to lead.

When a horse leads well, he will theoretically lead anywhere – which means that leading him into a trailer, for example, is not going to be an issue.

TEACHING THE HORSE TO LEAD WELL

☐ HOW TO DO IT

1 Look ahead, have some slack in the rope, and walk forwards. Vibrate the rope very softly in your hand as you go, so the horse is encouraged to come with you.

2 When he is moving with you, stop fairly abruptly, but without pulling on the rope, so if he doesn't stop to your body language, he will meet the end of the rope and it will stop him.

3 Repeat steps 1 and 2 a few times, and see how the horse becomes more attuned to your subtle signals; ultimately he follows your body language to 'go' and 'stop', meaning you don't have to do anything with the rope or your hands.

With a horse who leads well, you can really enjoy an experience of togetherness. You can lead the horse at any speed whilst the rope remains slack, because the horse is following your body language and focus.

PROBLEM SOLVING

If the horse pulls ahead of you Stop walking and plant yourself, so the horse bumps himself into the end of the rope. Once he stops, continue walking and repeat the exercise as necessary.

If the horse drags behind you Have a few feels on the rope in a forward direction, and if this doesn't speed up his feet, repeat it and touch him behind you with a long stick, making sure you keep your body facing the direction you want to go at all times.

If the horse refuses to move Lead his shoulders over to one side, so that his front legs have to start moving; then once he is moving, direct him the way you want to go.

The ultimate aim of training the horse to lead is that he leads well, whether you have a rope on him or not. In safe environments I like sometimes to test how much I am in partnership with the horse, or how much I am relying on the rope to get what I want.

If the horse barges into you Before the horse barges into you he will probably have looked away from you with his head, which then means his shoulder can easily barge you. Make sure the horse is looking straight ahead or slightly in your direction, by asking his head to come around with the rope, without looking at the horse. Take up more space yourself by expanding your body and, if necessary, walk with your elbow pointing in his direction so he jabs himself in the shoulder with the point of your elbow.

Alternatively, you can shake the rope in his direction to ask him to back off you – but this must be done without making him nervous or shy of you.

If the horse pulls away from you If the horse's head is turned slightly towards you, it is highly unlikely he will be able to pull away from you: his energy is more likely to be directed so that he comes around in front of you. But if he really does pull away habitually, work with him in a limited space such as a round pen or small paddock where he will not come to any harm and you can catch him each time he pulls away, so he learns it is pointless.

Something has excited Fantastique as I led her through the pasture. I have used my body language so that she stays out of my personal space. Without holding the rope tight I have also kept her head turned towards me so she cannot pull and run away.

Because she couldn't run away, the surge of power from her initial reaction has sent Fantastique airborne. The rope is slack, but she is still looking towards me with her head and moving her body away from me, so – despite the apparent drama – I am still in a reasonably safe position.

The mare has her feet back on the ground and is now looking to me for direction and reassurance.

SAFE AND PLEASANT TO BE AROUND

In my mind, a horse wouldn't be the perfect riding horse if he is great while you're on his back, but tries to kill you before and after you ride him!

Successful handling of horses is often a fine balance between being firm and being friendly, and that balance changes all the time with horses, depending on their mood, our emotional state, the environment or the weather. Being human, we don't always get the balance quite right between firmness and friendliness with horses, and it is something that we should be aware of for the whole of our lives around horses.

To give yourself and the horse the best chance of having a safe and pleasant time together, set things up for success. Teach the horse to lead well and stay out of your space, but also show him that grooming and tacking up are enjoyable parts of the process. Your relationship with your riding horse does not begin when you get on his back: you want him to be on your side before you get that far.

GROOMING

It is not uncommon for horses to be unhappy and even nervous about being groomed and handled. Each horse has a different sensitivity to its skin, and they always let you know, if you care to listen to them:

- Watch out for tail swishing, muzzle wrinkling, neck shaking, moving away from you, or the skin twitching. These are clear signs of disapproval or discomfort.
- Watch out for the horse relaxing his posture, resting a hind leg, for his bottom lip or eyes drooping, or his head dropping. These are all signs of pleasure and relaxation.
- It is a good idea to tie the horse up to groom him.
- Use the right brush for him: some horses need a soft brush or even just a gentle hand; some love a firm plastic curry comb on their coats.
- Use the time spent grooming to create trust and a better bond between you before you ride: this is a natural part of the horse's nature, and it is important to realize that one of the major ways horses affirm their bond with each other is by mutual grooming.
- Make sure the horse is standing well with his other three feet before picking up the fourth one.

TACKING UP

Tacking up is an integral part of the riding process, which means the way we tack up has a bearing on how the partnership between horse and rider will work.

When putting the bridle on, teach him to accept it willingly by taking your time and encouraging him to open his mouth for long enough that the bridle isn't hurried in and bangs on his teeth. Do this by tickling the side of his tongue through the corner of his mouth.

When saddling the riding horse, it is important to have his 'agreement' to wearing the saddle. By this I mean he should be happy about being saddled and girthed, as this is a part of the riding process, albeit before you actually sit astride him.

Assuming the saddle is a good fit, place the saddle on his back in a considerate way, not being timid or hesitant about it, but not banging it down on him, either. If the horse moves away at the sight or feel of the saddle he is probably telling you something of how he feels about it. If this is the case, hold the saddle in one hand and take a few moments to rub him on the neck and back with your spare hand, until you see him relax in his body a little, then proceed to place the saddle on his back.

When girthing the horse, I always girth up quite loosely to begin with, and will usually adjust the girth a couple more times before I get on. In any case, I don't normally tighten the girth any more than I would want someone tightening the belt on my trousers. It is easy to think that a tight girth is like a safety belt that will stop us from falling off the horse, but this is not the case: if we sit with balance we have every chance of staying on, loose girth or not.

Ideally the horse helps you to put the tack on!

Assuming it is in a safe space, I sometimes like to take the horse's tack off after riding and spend some time walking with him loose. I think this gives us both a chance to unwind and to reflect on the session we have just had.

STANDING STILL TO BE MOUNTED

I have noticed a direct link between a horse that stands well to be mounted and what he is like to ride. When a horse stands and waits with you at the mounting block he is more likely to stay 'with you' when he is being ridden, even at the canter… If he is sluggish coming up to the mounting block, he is often behind the leg when ridden. You could say that a horse not standing still to be mounted is not accepting his rider and therefore not really ready to be ridden.

Take time to teach him to stand and wait while you mount… you may want to adjust your clothing or maybe take a phone call before charging off across the wilderness! Teaching the horse to wait while you mount teaches him to 'wait' for you during the rest of your ride.

Backing Young Horses

When I am backing young horses, I teach them to stand to be mounted as part of the backing process, so the first time I ever sit astride the horse he is accepting me on his back and stands still and relaxed. This is a great way to begin building a trusting relationship with your future riding horse… of course it can take some time and patience.

☐ HOW TO DO IT

1 Use a mounting block without hard edges and site it where there is plenty of space (picture A).
2 Stand on the block and ask the horse to come alongside you, so the saddle is level with your body.
3 If he keeps moving around, away, or not lining himself up, stay calm and keep asking him, ideally so he ends up going round and round the mounting block in a small circle (pictures B and C). This is hard work for the horse, and he will soon wonder if standing still would be a better option.
4 Each time he passes the spot where you want him to stand, stroke him with your hand. If he stops at that spot, stroke him and pause (picture D).
5 Once he stands for you to mount, lean across and stroke his opposite shoulder, lean your weight on the top of the saddle with your free hand a few times and fiddle with the stirrup leather. If he still stands, have your reins at the right length in your rein hand on his neck, place your foot in the stirrup, place your free hand on

The mounting block has plenty of space surrounding it so the horse has room to keep moving around it should he wish to.

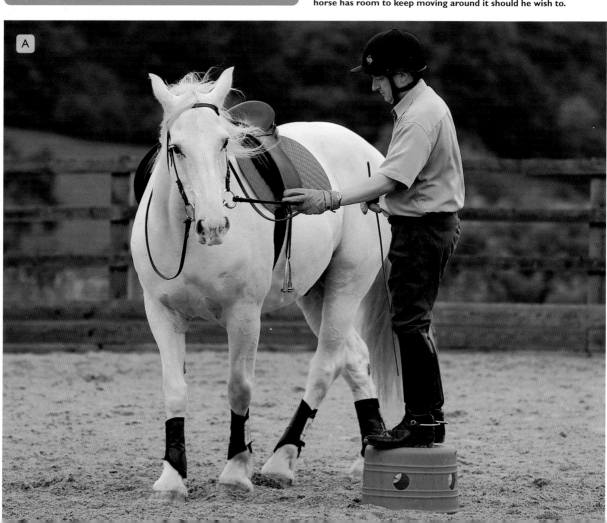

the opposite saddle flap, transferring your weight there, and begin to mount (picture E).

6 If he moves as you go to mount, step back on to the mounting block and repeat steps 3 to 5 until he is ready for another try.

7 Once you are finally in the saddle, use the reins and your voice to ask him to stand.

8 Pause and let him stand for a minute or so to enjoy the wonderful new standing-still trick he has learned.

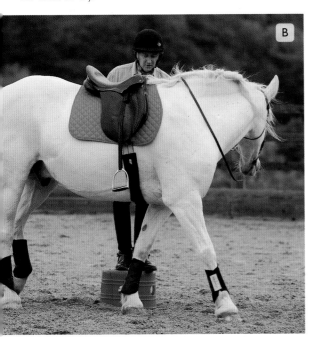

I am not trying to make Arnie stand still…

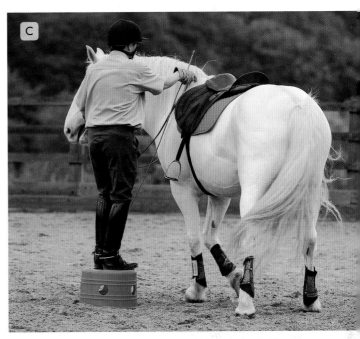

…I am waiting for him to figure out that it would be easier for him to stand still than to keep moving in small circles around me.

I want him to stand with the saddle close to me, so rather than bring his head around with the reins – which would move the saddle away from me – I rub him behind the saddle with my hand, which makes him want to move it closer.

When he finally stands and plants his weight over all four feet, I stroke him and proceed to mount, placing my weight on to his back gently and respectfully.

TEACHING THE HORSE TO BE 'STILL'

One of the things I have found to be very useful over the years is to teach the horse to be still, by standing in a particular spot on the ground. Once the horse accepts your asking him to stand still and be 'still', he will start to relax and to wait for you; this lowers his adrenalin level and enables him to be calm but attentive. Teaching him to be still when handled carries over very nicely into ridden work, too, so he learns to wait underneath you, rather than fidget when you ride him. With 'hot' or high energy horses I find this even more useful than with quiet horses.

Arnie likes to look around a lot with his head, so it has taken time to teach him to be 'still', as he is here.

☐ HOW TO DO IT

1 Make sure you are really quiet and still inside yourself.

2 Ask the horse to stand squarely in front of you on a particular spot.

3 If he moves, quietly place him back on the spot. Be prepared to do this for as long as it takes (the longest it took me was an afternoon!), and continue being quiet and completely patient.

4 If he looks around with his head, use the lead rope to quietly ask him to look straight towards you.

5 When the horse stands where you want and is still for a minute or two, stroke him, and then finish.

✓ **DOs**

- Notice little ways in which the horse steps over the politeness boundaries.
- Correct him in a calm, persistent way.

✗ **DON'Ts**

- Don't shout and wave your arms about.
- Don't set yourself up to be squashed or pushed around by a horse under any circumstances.

A Great Partner

When I ask people what their idea of the perfect riding horse is, one thing they say more than anything else is '*a great partner*'. Most people would agree that it is more satisfying, more fun, safer and you get much better results from a horse when he is a great partner.

By 'great partner' I mean a horse that works with you, who is willing and interested in what you do together, and you both thoroughly enjoy the time and companionship you share… Taking your partnership even further can mean your horse becomes a great friend and someone with whom you share a deep bond and connection, based on mutual respect, understanding and love.

In my mind, the perfect riding horse should definitely be a great partner. Whether you ride a cross-country course, dressage, show jumping, endurance, Western reining or pleasure class, or enjoy a quiet trip out in the countryside, one of the ultimate sensations for any rider is having a horse who is a great partner.

WORKING WITH THE HORSE'S NATURE

More and more people these days are thinking, talking and writing about working with the horse's nature. In reality, it makes no sense whatsoever to work against the horse's nature: he is a big, strong, fast, sensitive, reactive flight animal with a mind of his own and very powerful instincts to boost it all up with!

To work with the horse's nature means understanding things from his point of view, and patiently and intelligently working *with* him, rather than using force to get results. And the more we understand the true nature of horses – what makes them tick, what they like and dislike, how they think, feel and behave – the better equipped we are to create the kind of successful riding partner we wish for.

TEN TIPS FOR CREATING A GREAT PARTNERSHIP

1. Use the horse's natural inclination to be comfortable and to enjoy stimulation, variety and routine.

2. Stroke the horse a lot: horses use physical contact and mutual grooming to build bonds with each other. They find it pleasurable and reassuring, so as much as possible show the horse you care (picture A).

3. Reward often… it can be very easy for riders to notice all the things the horse does *wrong* and not notice what he does *right*. Training horses is far more effective if we build on what is right, rather than what is wrong.

   For students who only notice the 'wrongs' in their horse or themselves, I ask them to ride and say 'YES' out loud every moment they or the horse is doing something good. Much to their surprise, this usually results in them shouting an almost constant stream of 'YES's and the horse usually goes better than it has ever gone before, without the rider changing anything else!

4. Do things the horse likes. If he likes jumping, jump; if he likes galloping through the forest, head for the forest (picture B). If he likes sucking the end of the hosepipe, let him. If he loves having his ears scratched, rub his ears.

The best way to develop an all-round riding horse for any purpose is to give him plenty of variety in his work. Combining school work with riding outdoors helps the horse to improve physically and mentally.

5. Make sure the horse is well cared for. Meet his physical, mental, social and emotional needs in his life away from you. To me it is essential that horses live with others whose companionship they enjoy. Take a 'holistic' approach: if he's happy at home he'll probably be happy at work, and if he's not happy at home he probably won't be happy at work… just like us, really.

6. Only work on one thing at a time, and take one small step at a time … So if you are working on the horse's flexibility, don't worry for a moment if you lose the precision of the circle; or if you start working on lateral movements, don't worry for a moment if the horse loses impulsion.

7. Keep it interesting, so the horse remains awake and stimulated by what he is doing: for example, if he spends four days in the arena and his flatwork goes 'flat', do something different on day five, such as taking him riding outside (picture C), or jumping.

   Even within your routine you can add some variety: every day your flatwork can be different, one day warming up in walk, maybe another day warming up in an easy trot, or working on the lunge or in hand.

8. Be trustworthy and 'emotionally centred' around the horse at all times: don't shout, move quickly, get bad tempered or frustrated, as it makes him nervous and undermines your leadership role. That sounds very easy to say, I know, but it can be easy to do, too, if you make sure you work within your own and the horse's comfort zone.

9. Show him what you want in ways he understands, so he is not confused. Horses like an easy life and are generally willing to please (picture D), so if you can make the right things easy, it is almost the only skill you will ever need to train a horse. From his first few steps under the rider to sequences of flying changes, make it easy for him and he will probably just do it for you.

10. Give him time… lots of time.

Doing things the horse likes to do is important for developing a great partnership and having a happy horse.

TOUCHING THE HORSE'S BODY

When we groom the horse we may well brush him all over his body, but there can be more to touching the horse's body than the merely functional process of getting him clean.

Before riding the horse, it is sometimes worth taking a couple of minutes to touch each area of the horse with the hands; that means on top, underneath and on his right and left sides. It means touching him everywhere, from his muzzle all the way back to his tail and hind feet.

Doing this can settle the horse and help him to relax.

It also tells me where he might be tense or nervous. For example, if he is tense about his hindquarters he may be more likely to react by rushing forwards if something startles him when I ride him. Another example is, if he is not comfortable about his muzzle being stroked all around he may not be happy to 'give' me his mouth when I ride, and instead may resist the action of the bit or toss his head. Stroking the horse's body also helps to create a connection with the horse before I climb on his back, and builds trust.

It also puts the horse 'into' his body. What I mean is, it makes him aware of his own body, and connects neural pathways from his brain to each part of his body that I touch. This can be a great help when riding, as I will want to influence and 'talk' to different parts of his body through the aids when I ride.

The horse's flank is another sensitive area. I have been checking Aurora's expression and noting she has raised her head slightly, letting me know she is not sure about my touching her there. However, I will politely and rhythmically continue stroking her here until she relaxes. Horses who are either over-sensitive or unresponsive to the rider's leg can really benefit from being stroked in this area.

This is an inexperienced horse called Aurora. She can be quite reactive, so I need to form an especially trusting partnership with her for our ridden work. Here I am stroking her muzzle, nose and mouth gently, until she accepts my hands without moving. When I ride, I want her to accept my guidance without reacting when I use the reins on her nose (hackamore) or mouth (bit), so it is important she is happy about me touching her there first. Horses who react to the bridle by evading the bit or tossing their heads can benefit from being stroked in this area.

Aurora is a horse who can react by going forwards very fast when she is worried, so it is very worthwhile creating a connection with her hind legs by stroking and touching them. I have carefully worked my way back here, making sure I won't get kicked. You can see by her expression that she has relaxed nicely. Horses who react by running forwards under saddle are often over-sensitive about their hind legs and back end, so it is worth spending time getting them to relax in this area.

INTRODUCING THE HORSE TO EQUIPMENT

To have a great partner, we need him to trust us, and that includes trusting us with all the equipment we will be using, for example ropes, saddle, bridle and sticks.

Some horses are naturally suspicious about equipment, but most are pretty relaxed about it, unless it has caused them some kind of discomfort, pain or fright. Actually, horses are less worried about the equipment itself than they are about the intention or body language of the person wielding it, so we need to become as aware as possible about how we move when we handle equipment near horses… I am not suggesting creeping around, but I do suggest you avoid moving in jerky or threatening ways.

INTRODUCING THE HORSE TO A STICK

☐ HOW TO DO IT

1 Stand with a passive body posture and avoid facing the horse directly.
2 Starting with his neck or shoulders, stroke the horse with the stick, making sure your movements are slow and rhythmical (picture A).
3 The aim is to have him stand still and relax, and not move his feet around. You want to reassure him that you are safe to be around when you have a stick in your hand.
4 If he does move when you stroke him, quietly follow him and continue to stroke him rhythmically with the stick until he stops moving, and then immediately stop stroking. Relax yourself for a minute or two before beginning again.

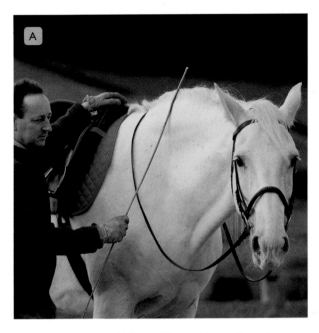

I will stroke him all over his body with the stick so he knows he can trust me with it anywhere.

5 Once the horse is comfortable, stroke different areas of his body (picture B).
6 Do the same thing with any ropes or other equipment you will want to use, again with a very passive body position and expression.

I am stroking the horse's hind legs to teach him not to be afraid of the stick.

TEACHING THE HORSE THE LANGUAGE OF THE AIDS

To have a great partner, you need to have a means of communication that works extremely well, and for the riding horse that means of communication is normally in the form of 'the aids'.

Traditionally, the aids are the physical requests or signals we give to the horse via the seat, reins, legs and voice to ask him to do what we want.

Horses are creatures that naturally move into pressure, yet the aids we use to ride require the horse to move *away* from pressure – for example moving forwards away from the legs, yielding or slowing to the bit – so we have to gradually attune him to the idea of moving away from pressure. Principally we teach him to move away from the 'pressure' of an aid by repeating or increasing the intensity of the aid until he responds, at which point we cease the aid: so when he responds to our request, he effectively gains comfort, release or a 'bit of peace'.

Every aid begins with an idea, a thought of what we want from the horse, and that is often enough to have him respond. Maybe you have experienced those moments with horses yourself sometimes.

The physical aids are ways to influence – not force – the horse to carry out our ideas, and that is why they should always start incredibly lightly. Horses are very sensitive, and when they are listening and understand our aids, the aids can be almost non-existent and will get the response we want – often better than strong aids, actually.

Probably the most important element in getting the right response from the aids with lightness is timing our aids correctly. This is something which takes a bit of time and effort to learn, but the result of learning to time the aids well is amazing.

In simple terms, you can think of the right rein being connected to the horse's right foreleg; the left rein connected to his left foreleg; your right leg and the right side of your seat connected to the horse's right hind leg, and your left leg and seat being connected to his left hind leg. The best moment to use any of those connections is to give the aid via your rein or leg when the horse's corresponding leg is just leaving the ground; for example:

- to give an effective rein aid with your right rein, give it as the right foreleg is just leaving the ground;
- to give an effective leg aid with your left leg, use it just as the left hind foot is leaving the ground.

Perfect rider checklist

Give the horse time to respond to an aid. If he doesn't respond, repeat the aid a little more strongly. As soon as the horse responds, the aid must cease: that is good training… even better is to cease the aid when you *know* the horse is going to respond: that is *great* training. The horse doesn't really learn the aids by them being applied, he actually learns by them ceasing, and the rider leaving him alone for a moment.

Look at this picture of Arnie and see the connection between my inside (right) leg and his inside hind leg; my outside (left) leg and Arnie's outside leg; the inside (right) rein and Arnie's inside foreleg; and the outside rein with his outside (left) foreleg. As you look at the picture, imagine also the connection between the left and right sides of my seat and the left and right sides of Arnie's back. Notice how our heads are aligned, too. All these different connections are helping to create a living partnership in motion between two very different creatures: horse and human.

EXPLORING YOUR PARTNERSHIP THROUGH LIBERTY WORK

I turn the horse loose, and if he runs away (as Fantastique did here), I let him run. While he moves away from me I look at him and quietly move towards him. If he turns and looks at me or steps towards me a little, I step back, creating a space for him to come to me, should he choose to.

I like to turn my horses loose in a safe, enclosed environment to explore what kind of relationship we have and to have a conversation with the horse using body language. Doing this is an opportunity to find out what he really thinks of working with me. It is a chance to meet him on equal terms and talk to him in his own language, without using reins, lead ropes or attaching any other kind of equipment.

If the horse runs off and shows no desire to interact with me when I turn him loose, I have a good idea I need to work on our relationship. If he stays with me, I know he will be 'with me' when I ride him, and if he starts playing rough horse games or charging at me, I know I need to address some leadership issues!

I continue with this process of stepping towards him when he moves away, and giving him invitations to come to me when his focus is aimed my way. By stepping back, I draw him towards me until he is standing next to me.

I then stroke him and am friendly. Horses reward one another by allowing each other to stand close in their space, then letting each other have a bit of peace: this is what I am doing here, in addition to stroking the horse in a gentle way.

NOTE: If the horse is quite dominant, I use a positive body posture (as in the picture) and do not give him ground so readily, as this can invite him to run at me.

✓ DOs

- Show him the way… if you want the horse to be a great partner for you, you have to be a great partner for him.

✗ DON'Ts

- Don't forget the horse is a living creature, not a machine (he will really appreciate it if you can remember that).
- Don't forget to put some time and thought into the kind of relationship you are creating with your horse by what you do with him and the way you are when he is around.

Listens to the Rider

One of the cornerstones of any great horse and rider partnership is how much they listen to each other. When the horse is focused and attentive to his rider, he responds to the rider's aids, thoughts and subtle suggestions as if by magic. To the onlooker, it appears as though the horse reads the rider's mind and the two are connected in body and mind – perhaps even soul – in a seamless dance, as if they have become one.

At the opposite end of the spectrum, when the horse is not listening to the rider, they can get into all manner of difficulties and even danger.

In order to keep the horse listening, the rider also needs to 'listen' constantly to the horse, especially in new situations. By noticing immediately when something begins to bother the horse, or when his attention starts to wander, the rider has a relatively small job to do to ask the horse to listen to him again. But if the rider is not concentrating on the horse, the horse's attention may wander away so much that he forgets he even has a rider!

Having a horse that doesn't listen is a big issue for a lot of riders, and when the horse doesn't listen, there is very little chance of him responding well to the aids, forming a great partnership, or performing to his potential.

LISTENING ON THE GROUND

As with many aspects of creating the perfect riding horse, the job of encouraging the horse to listen to you begins on the ground. When your horse listens to you on the ground, you can be sure that he is more likely to listen to you when you ride him, too.

Whenever you are around the horse on the ground – whether you are leading him, grooming him, tacking him up, in the stable with him, or when you are near him in the field – always be aware of where his attention is. You can tell this by his ear position and, more easily, by where his head is looking. Despite having nearly 360-degree vision, horses almost always turn their heads in the direction of whatever catches their attention. If the horse's ears or head are pointing away from you, it is fairly accurate to assume that he is not listening to you.

Horses weigh about half a ton (in fact I should think Arnie weighs about three-quarters of a ton!) and their reactions are very fast, so I want my horse to be looking at and listening to me whenever I am around him – and I can encourage this by making sure that his head is always turned very slightly towards me. I *never* want my horses walking on me, forgetting I am there, or barging into me, in any way so I always pay attention to where the horse's attention is and ask him to look at me by giving little feels on the lead rope.

A horse is a big powerful animal – especially a horse like **Arnie** – so whether we are riding, leading or even just being around the horse, it is nice to know he is aware of us and 'listening'. Here Arnie is at liberty and moving around me, but you can see clearly by his expression and the position of his ears that he is listening to my body language and gestures, as if he is waiting for me to give him his next direction.

I am distracted fiddling with the rope. You can see by Arnie's head, body posture and ears that his attention has gone off over the hedge and he is not really listening to me. This puts me in a vulnerable position. With his head turned away, he is starting to barge into me with his shoulder and could easily knock me down (picture 1).

Perry's Tips

To ask a horse to listen to you, use the rope or reins to ask him very simply and clearly to turn his head slightly towards you. If he looks away again (which he probably will), repeat the request... as many times as is necessary.

I am fully attentive again, and by using the rope to ask him to look slightly towards me with his head, Arnie has remembered I am there and relaxed his posture (picture 2).

TEACHING THE HORSE TO LISTEN UNDER SADDLE

As we have already said, it is essential that the rider 'listens' to the horse at all times. When riding, you should be able to feel when the horse ceases to be soft to the aids and should notice if his attention starts to drift with indications such as his head or his ear position. You may also feel the horse's body or back become rather tense, or his rhythm become a little irregular.

To have the horse listen to you when you are riding in the arena – just like on the ground – ask his head to be straight or turned very slightly to the inside of the school using the inside rein and a light inside leg at the girth.

Arnie is one of those horses who likes to look at everything that is going on in the world, and it can be quite a challenge to keep his attention on me, even in the arena. Here he is wondering what is happening beyond the fence, and is forgetting I am riding him. Once the horse forgets you are there, he is a split second away from reacting instinctively to something 'scary' and taking flight. If he knows you are there guiding him, he is more likely to listen to you and stay 'with you' by responding to your aids.

I have asked Arnie to look slightly to the inside of the arena using light feels on the inside rein and inside leg. This has brought his attention back to me and he is relaxing. Always be attentive to where the horse is putting his attention, because if he is not listening to you, you can be quite vulnerable. The other great thing about the horse listening to you is that he can also relax, because he doesn't have to worry, take responsibility or be the leader any more.

Perry's Tip

If a horse is really inattentive, and asking his head to look inwards doesn't work, whether in the arena or outside, try riding lots of small patterns and circles with frequent changes of direction, so he has to listen and concentrate on his balance. Use as light a contact and legs as soft as possible while still asking him to turn his head in the direction he is going at all times. Having quiet legs and hands is more effective than holding him tight, which can result in increasing his levels of energy and anxiety.

LISTENING WHEN OUT RIDING

Whenever and wherever you ride, try to have some kind of conversation with your horse most of the time – for example, where he is looking with his head or what tempo you want in walk, trot or canter. Maybe ask for a halt, small circle or reinback occasionally to remind him you are there. In **picture 1**, I have asked Fantastique to halt and pause for a moment to regain her attention… she is listening now, but you can see by the way she is leaning forwards, even in this halt, that she was getting ahead of me and needed reminding I was there!

Once the horse is really listening to you in halt, walk and trot outdoors, then you have a much better chance of keeping him listening in the canter, too. In **picture 2** Fantastique is full of energy and the canter is quite springy, but her ear position shows she is still listening and waiting for my directions.

To get the horse's attention on you when riding outdoors – even on a straight track – imagine that you still have an 'inside' rein and an 'outside' rein, as you would in the arena. Use the 'inside' rein (and inside leg) to ask him to look slightly one way – ideally away from whatever else is drawing his attention. This gives you the opportunity to continue having a quiet conversation and keep him listening. In **picture 3**, even though we are walking a straight line across open ground, I am imagining Fantastique and I are on the 'left' rein and I am asking her to bend a little to the left for a few strides. When I feel her relax her mind and body, I will release the aids and let her walk straight again.

It should not be necessary to be 'on the horse's case' all the time in order to have him listening to you. What I look for with any aspect of training or riding my horses is to be able to leave them in peace as much as possible, which means taking every opportunity – when they are doing what I want – to allow them to relax. In **picture 4** the mare is walking nicely on a loose rein, however she is still listening to me: although it is a chance for both of us to relax, I am by no means asleep in the saddle, and she is still listening and by no means asleep on her feet!

Asking the horse for the occasional halt outdoors reminds him you are there, and teaches him to 'wait' for you.

Even when riding on a straight line, it can sometimes be useful to imagine having an 'inside' and 'outside'. Here I am asking Fantastique to bend a little to the left, as a way of having a conversation with her and reaffirming that she is light to the aids.

Once the horse is accustomed to listening in the slower paces, it should be possible to have him listen just as well in the canter and gallop.

Even on a loose rein in a relaxed walk, I still want the horse listening and aware of me.

Perry's Tips

- If the horse is not listening to your aids, ride lots of transitions and count the exact number of strides of each gait: for example ten trot, five walk, ten trot, five walk, and so on. You can do this outside or in the arena. If he is too quiet, do this exercise in the higher gaits (trot and canter); if he is too 'hot' and lively, do the exercise in the lower gaits (walk and halt).
- If your horse becomes so agitated when ridden that you can no longer communicate with him, it can help him to settle and listen to you again if you dismount and lead him for a while (assuming he leads well!). Having you by his side where he can see he has a companion should give him more confidence.

RIDING IN COMPANY

One of the common problems with riding out in company is that horses tend to listen to each other rather than listen to their riders. This is more likely to happen the faster the pace and the more horses that are present. To help the horse listen to you more, if possible take him out with perhaps just one other horse, and spend as much time as necessary in walk and steady trots to settle him. When he is able to listen to you in those circumstances, add one or two more horses, or start asking for a few easy canters. Eventually you should be able to gallop across open country with a bunch of other horses and still have him listening to you, rather than forgetting you are on board and letting his instinct to run with the herd take over!

It is important to teach the horse to go in front and behind other horses in company and still listen to the rider. Some horses are naturally easier when they are ridden in the front, and some are easier when ridden behind. This is simply down to their individual nature. With patience, most horses will gradually accept going first or last in a group.

To help with this, take turns to halt while the other horse rides just a few yards past; you stop and they ride past; they stop and you ride past, and so on (this can be done with one or more horses). Begin this exercise in walk, and as the horses get the idea of it and improve, try overtaking each other in trot and eventually in canter, while the other horse stays calmly in walk.

Here Arnie is being asked to stand still while I ride past him. In a few yards I will halt my horse and Arnie will ride past me.

Always be quiet and thoughtful when working with the horse on the lunge, to build his trust and confidence in you, and because it is important to make sure you are both friends and enjoy working together.

LUNGEING

There are lots of different opinions about lungeing, and lots of ways to do it. Done thoughtfully, it has many uses: to teach the horse to listen to us and follow our directions, to develop a partnership before we ride him, and to warm up and strengthen his body. Lungeing done very well is an art, and could be – and often is – the subject of a whole book in itself.

Lungeing is *not* simply a case of making the horse run round in circles with us standing in the middle; it should be carried out in a very quiet way with empathy and thoughtfulness. A horse running frantically in circles is not listening properly to his handler – at least not in the way we wish it to.

Begin by teaching the horse to lead very well. If he will go and stop obediently and is physically mature enough (I don't lunge horses until they are four years old), he is ready to begin lungeing.

With your lunge line in one hand and whip resting casually in the other, stand with the horse, talk softly to him and stroke his neck. When you are ready to ask him to move off, make sure you face the direction you want him to go with your body, and if at all possible, DO NOT step backwards to give him room. When we lunge the horse we want him to be moving forwards to our body language and driving aids; if we step backwards even a little, we invite him to come into us, rather than moving off away from us.

Look in the direction you want him to go, say 'walk on' in an enthusiastic tone, maybe click your tongue, tap his hind legs lightly with the whip, and perhaps begin walking slowly forwards yourself. Remember to think of sending him on in front of you, not just making him go round and round you in a circle, otherwise you may find it difficult for him to go away from you at all.

THE BENEFITS OF LUNGEING

Lungeing helps to build listening skills between you and the horse, and assists the horse in finding his rhythm and balance. It helps you to find out how the horse is feeling, and to look at how he is moving. You can also get an idea of how he will feel to ride. How he is on the lunge line will give an idea of how he will be with the reins, and his responsiveness and acceptance of the lunge whip will give an indication of how he will be with your leg aids.

Lungeing can be tiring for the horse, so it is important only to do what the horse can comfortably manage for his level of ability and fitness. It is also important to change the rein/direction frequently.

LUNGEING EQUIPMENT

I use a simple halter and lunge line, brushing boots if the horse is shod, and place the snaffle bridle *underneath* the halter. The line is attached to the halter, on the left or right side according to which rein I am lungeing on, and like

this plays the same role as an 'open rein' when I ride (see 'Excellent Steering', page 68).

The handler should carry a lunge whip, but it is important to use the whip very calmly and carefully (see Lungeing Tips on page 48).

When appropriate I use side-reins, but they are always introduced and used with discretion, and used too long, rather than too short. I prefer to use side-reins quite loose to give the horse something to reach forwards into, rather than using them to 'set' the horse's head position.

NOTE: It is essential not to shorten the side-reins too much, as this puts the horse in a position where he hollows his frame and so cannot use his back properly. The side-reins should always be adjusted to the same length on both sides of the horse.

Always wear suitable footwear yourself while lungeing, as well as gloves, in case the horse does something unpredictable and pulls the lunge rein through your hand.

Although I would usually begin the lungeing session quietly in walk, Arnie has decided to spend a few moments using this session to let off steam! If the horse is too wild or uncontrollable on the lunge, I shorten the line and walk almost next to him so I can control the situation, rather like leading him, instead of standing in the middle and having him run off all over the place.

2

Arnie has settled into a good shape and rhythm in the trot, reaching nicely through his top line and listening well. I am facing slightly in the direction he is going, and being quite passive in the centre of the circle. I am holding the line as I would a rein, with the stick trailing behind him to ask him to step forwards when necessary.

LUNGEING TIPS

The handler should use light 'feels' or vibrations of the hand to communicate to the horse with the lunge line, and should carry and use the lunge whip very calmly and carefully, so the horse accepts the messages it gives to go forwards without becoming nervous and afraid of the whip or the handler. I prefer to use the stick more behind the horse than towards the hindquarters, because pointing the stick at the hindquarters can push them outwards on the circle, which means the horse goes crooked. What we want is for the horse to go on a precise circle where his hind feet follow the same track as his fore feet, and we want his rhythm and balance to be nice and regular.

With little 'feels' on the lunge line to ask him to look very slightly into the circle, and subtle use of the stick to ask him to step forwards, he can be brought into a nice shape. The timing of the stick is important, and it is used in the same way as our inside leg when we ride, which is when the inside hind leg is just leaving the ground and beginning its forward step. If you time the stick this way, the horse will take a deeper step with his hind leg and work into a better shape.

3

Now Arnie is settled and working well I have introduced the side-reins. Notice he is putting some slack in the side-reins, which are adjusted to be reasonably long anyway. The forward impulsion from behind is coming up through his back and raising his front nicely. Look at the lovely steps he is taking with his hind legs, enabling his front legs to stretch out in longer strides and making his overall shape more beautiful. Notice how my hand holding the line is in the same position as for holding the reins when riding.

✔ DOs
- Pay attention all the time to where the horse is putting his attention.
- Always be patient, and ask as many times as is necessary for him to listen to you.

✗ DON'Ts
- Don't forget it only takes a split second for a horse who isn't listening to you to do something that takes you by surprise.
- Don't forget the horse likes you to be his leader, which means asking him to listen.

Calm, Willing and Forward-Going

Horses are amazing creatures, full of energy, rhythm, speed and movement, and when we ride them it enables us to share the joys and thrills of their incredible qualities. In order to share those joys and thrills as we wish, we need to teach the horse to give us the amount of willingness, tempo and energy we ask for.

The terms 'willing', 'forward-going' and 'impulsion' are used a great deal around riding horses, and are often taken to mean the horse goes forwards without the rider having to ask him to. For my perfect riding horse, I certainly want him to be willing and forward-going and to have impulsion from the lightest of aids – that's true – but I also want him to go forwards at *my* speed and with the amount of energy *I* request, *not more and not less*: wherever he is, whatever job he is doing, in walk, trot and canter… To me that is the true meaning of the term 'impulsion'.

When you sit on a willing riding horse and he gives you just what you ask for, the experience of directing all that harnessed, available energy with lightness is fantastic.

TEACHING THE HORSE TO BE CALM

About 20 years ago I saw a well-known Western trainer giving a demonstration with one of his young horses at an equestrian trade fair. Some of the other expert demonstrators had struggled with their horses in the noise and bustle of the situation, but this trainer's horse stood quite happily while he sat astride it and talked to the audience. Then he picked up a lope (canter) from halt, performed a flying change, whizzed around the short side, another flying change, halted at X, the horse went back to dozing and the trainer carried on talking to the audience. I thought to myself, 'That's what I want from my horses': that they are willing to switch off as well as switch on. Most people can get a horse to switch on or hot up, but how many can get them to switch off, too?

Although horses like to play, generally speaking they are laid-back creatures who like to save their energy. This makes sense to a prey animal: he needs to exercise to be fit enough to run fast should he be threatened by a predator, but he also needs to have plenty of reserve energy in the tank should he need it for escaping danger.

Unfortunately, what happens with a great many horses when we ride them is that their natural tendency to conserve energy gets lost in their anxiety, tension or over-excitement. It then becomes difficult to control and direct the amount of energy we get, and it can even become difficult to control the horse at all, as I am sure many of you have experienced from time to time.

Unless the horse is calm, he is not likely to listen very well to his rider, nor will he use himself in the best possible way. Whilst it can be fun to ride a horse with bags of energy, impulsion is something that should be asked for by the rider, rather than the rider trying to keep the lid on it like an over-boiling pan of hot soup! Since being laid-back is their natural state, a calm horse is a happy horse.

I will often lead the horse around the arena before riding to establish a calm basis for our work together, as well as to increase the horse's trust and confidence in me. Doing this also gives me the chance to have an emotional 'weather check' to see how the horse is feeling. The horse's brain and eyesight is quite separate on the left and right, so it is important to do this on both reins.

☐ HOW TO DO IT

- Make sure you are calm yourself inside. Horses are very sensitive to our emotions, so it is important that we give them the right messages by being genuinely calm inside ourselves whenever we are around them. To give yourself the best chance of being calm inside, take your time with everything, and work with the horse within your comfort zone, gradually expanding it as you become more and more confident.

- Take your time when mounting (as seen previously), so that the horse already has to slow down his thinking.

- Don't allow the horse to move off before you are ready: if he moves, use an open rein (see 'Excellent Steering' page 68) to quietly guide him in a very small circle until he is exactly where he was when you mounted. You should repeat this if necessary.

- Spend time in between exercises (or when riding outside) simply just sitting on the horse doing nothing, other than perhaps talking to him or rubbing his withers (doing nothing very well is actually quite difficult). I have quite often sat in the centre of the arena on a young horse whilst giving a riding lesson. The horse soon learns that he can relax, because we may be doing nothing for quite some time.

- Horses are naturally calmer when their heads are low, and more tense when their heads are high. It helps therefore to spend time whilst riding allowing the horse to stretch his head and neck forwards and down, especially in walk on a long rein and at halt.

- If the horse is not calm in his walk, ask him to ride a small pattern such as a figure of eight or a serpentine until you feel him relax in his body, at which point stop and do nothing for a few minutes, then begin walking again. It is important that the rein and leg aids are present but light, so they support the horse by being there, but do not wind him up by building or collecting his energy.

- A horse should be able to walk, trot and canter, do flying changes and jump, all with calmness. If he starts to lose his calmness in what you are doing – for example, he becomes too excited in canter – go back a couple of stages to riding in walk until he settles.

- Remember that horses are creatures of habit, so if you habitually try to dissipate his excess energy by running it off him in order to get to a point where he is calmer, you may accidentally have taught him the habit of running around being highly energetic, rather than teaching him the habit of calmness.

Although Fantastique is alert, she remains calm and happy to stand and wait until I ask her to move on. It is worth taking horses out into different situations, meeting different creatures and taking time out like this, so they learn to relax and don't think they need to be busy all the time.

TEACHING THE HORSE TO GO FORWARDS

☐ HOW TO DO IT

1 Have a clear idea and intention in your mind about going forwards – at what speed, and where you want to go.

2 Release and free your inner thigh and pelvis a little. Relaxing the thigh and pelvis allows the horse to move, and teaches him to listen to your body. He will eventually go forwards just from feeling your 'release'. (Another advantage of doing this is that it creates space for him to lift and come up through his back as he goes forwards.)

The thigh should be nice and relaxed to allow the horse's back and ribs to move and expand, but also this enables the rider's lower leg to lie gently on the horse's sides, encouraging forward movement without lots of effort on the rider's part. Often, sluggish horses will go forwards *more* to a very light leg touching the hairs on their sides than they will to a rider who kicks and squeezes all the time, which only serves to make horses dull to the leg.

I am relaxing the inner thigh and allowing my lower leg to hang down the horse's side; this asks and releases the horse to go forwards freely, without me getting in his way and making it more difficult for him to do so.

3 Touch him incredibly lightly on his sides with the lower leg (horses are *so* sensitive they can feel a fly land on them!). The light touch on his sides triggers a nerve response in the horse, which activates muscles connected to his hind leg, causing him to take a deeper, longer step forwards.

4 To support the light leg, in the beginning the horse may need a couple of light touches of the stick on his hindquarters to help him understand what you want… I use two touches: 'tap-tap'… the first tap says to the horse *'I'm going to touch you with the stick for more forwardness,'* and the second touch asks him for more forwardness.

NOTE: The stick should *never* be used to punish or even surprise the horse as it ruins his rhythm, balance and trust. If your horse is too afraid of the stick for you to be able to use it, take some time to desensitize him to this very useful tool from the ground (see 'A Great Partner', page 26). Even a tap done too strongly can disturb the horse's rhythm by surprising him, and if he reacts with surprise at all, it tells you that you need to be lighter with the stick.

Perry's Tip

When horses are 'willing', it means they give us the energy we ask for without us having to work hard to get it. To help the horse to be willing, we need to make it as easy as possible for him to give us his energy, which means we stop 'pushing' him. Instead, we find a way to educate the horse to willingly give us his energy…Remember it is *his* willing energy we want; we can't 'create' that energy by dragging it out of him.

5 Be sure you are sitting in balance (not tipping your body backwards or forwards and therefore not being behind or in front of the horse's forward movement). Your body and seat should be willing to go forwards with the horse as he moves. This has the effect of saying 'YES' to the horse, and lets him know that you want him to go.

6 Only repeat steps 1 to 4 if, or when, the horse lets his energy decrease or the tempo slows down.

Even at a flat-out gallop, where there is an incredible amount of forward movement, it is important that we stay with the horse's centre of gravity and balance as he surges forwards.

A universal riding myth

Kicking or squeezing the horse's sides with your legs is the way many of us are taught to get horses to go forwards. This method is not really correct. It is true that most horses will go forwards a little more when you do this because they have been conditioned to do it, but they do it in half measure and without fluidity because it is not a natural reaction for the horse… in fact, many young horses simply do not understand this type of aid at all, and some react to the rider kicking or squeezing by bucking at the discomfort caused.

The other drawback with kicking or squeezing the horse to ask him to go forwards is that, in order to kick or squeeze (even a little bit) with the lower leg, the rider has to tighten or brace their thigh or pelvis, which actually makes it *more difficult* for the horse to go forwards. We are therefore asking the horse to 'go' and 'not go' at the same time, and then wondering why he isn't willing; it's a bit like driving a car with one foot on the accelerator and one foot on the brake at the same time.

STICKS AND SPURS

Personally I find the stick to be a very useful tool for communication with the horse, especially when it is used to give light touches at the right moment in time, but it should NEVER, NEVER be used harshly or for punishment.

The sticks I usually use are hazel branches that I find growing in the forest. The advantage of picking my own sticks is that I can cut any length needed. For most of this book I am using a stick cut to about 1.2m, which is a comfortable length for me to touch the horse's hindquarters from the saddle without disturbing my hands on the reins. This is further helped by the stick being slightly bent, so it curves inwards towards the horse a little at its tip.

The stick or whip receives a lot of 'bad press', and in many cases, quite rightly so, but used with sensitivity it is a very useful means of communication with the horse.

The spur can be used so subtly that you can lift just a couple of hairs on the horse's flank as a very refined alternative to a leg aid.

Spurs are not ideal for asking the horse to go faster or more forwards; rather they are useful for more collection, lift or bend, and they should be used very sensitively to refine the intimate leg aids that take place between a more advanced horse and his rider.

Perry's Tip

To tune the horse up to the leg, only use your legs to get a forward response; never use them repeatedly without getting a reaction from the horse… if you want the horse to be 'in front of the leg' he must respond to every leg aid you give, which means you should not keep giving leg aids every stride to ask the horse to 'keep going'. If the horse slackens you ask for more forwardness with a light leg, maybe a 'tap-tap' with the stick, then leave him alone as he goes more forwards again.

Perfect Rider Checklist

The Body and Seat

It is not ideal to *push* actively with the seat, as this can make you stiffen your loins, which impedes the horse's movement. Active pushing can also press the horse's back down, rather than allowing it to come up. Instead of pushing, release and allow with your seat. When the rider pushes, it trains the horse to be lazy: when the rider releases it trains the horse to look for space, it becomes easy for him to move forwards, and he becomes more sensitive to the rider's seat.

The rider's seat allows and *goes with* the horse's movement… avoid bracing or being left behind as this will train the horse to slow down, perhaps when you don't want him to.

EXERCISES FOR GOING AT THE RIDER'S SPEED

Horses that go too slowly are withholding their energy, and horses that go too fast are running out from under the rider, instead of 'working through', so it is critical that the horse should go at the rider's speed. When a horse goes forwards at the rider's speed he is more likely to be working his body and hindquarters and balancing himself in partnership with the rider, both physically and mentally.

Rather than having to pull the reins to slow down, or use your legs constantly to go faster, the perfect riding horse should pick up the tempo from your thoughts and almost non-existent signals from your body, which means he will go forwards at your speed with the minimum of aids.

Instead of relying so much on the aids, we can teach him to respond to our subtle signals by using different patterns and exercises to get what we want (see below and following pages), and let the patterns or exercises do the work of making the horse more responsive.

The horse is nicely 'under my seat' and going at my speed. The results of her going at my speed are that it is easier for me to stay with her, and she is working well from behind.

WHEN THE HORSE GOES TOO SLOWLY

As you practise using the sequence of aids described in the section 'Teaching the Horse to go Forwards' on page 52 in a consistent and conscious way, you should find your horse getting more and more responsive to your leg aids.

With a horse that lacks impulsion, it can easily happen that the rider ends up working very hard to get him going or keep him going. However, it should not be necessary to do this when we ride, as you will see in the section on page 58 'Some ways to get more forwardness'.

But before considering what we can do to get the horse to give us more impulsion, there are two essential points for the rider.

1. Intention

Impulsion largely comes from the rider's intention or the power of his/ her mind. If the rider has a clear intention to GO, GO, GO, then the horse is more likely to GO. Intention is not the same thing as hoping: it means having a clear idea of what tempo you want and being committed to getting it, from the very first stride through to the very last. You may have seen a 'lazy' horse go really slowly for one rider and faster for another, without either rider looking much different – but the difference is in the clarity of their intention.

2. Balance

One of the things that can really slow a horse down is if the rider sits out of balance and is therefore stiff in their body and legs. By 'sitting in balance' I mean not tipping even the

Arnie could easily be the type of horse to go too slowly in order to save himself from having to work. This picture captures one of those moments where the horse goes too slowly and the rider ends up being tempted to push, use strong legs, or get quite braced in their attempts to make the horse go forwards more… and you can see me starting to do those things here. Notice how, when this horse goes too slowly, he is heavy on his forehand and not taking very deep steps with his hind legs.

slightest bit backwards or forwards. When the rider sits in perfect vertical balance with the horse, it frees up the rider's body, which in turn frees up the horse's body and allows him to move forwards more freely.

SOME TIPS TO GET MORE FORWARDNESS

• Firstly have the horse's teeth, tack and back checked to make sure he is not going too slowly because of physical discomfort or pain.

• Ride lots of straight lines and big circles. Avoid tight turns or small circles, especially when changing direction, as this can slow the horse down.

• Do lots of snappy transitions up and down the paces; for example, if the walk or trot are too slow, have a quick canter, then go back to walk or trot. Try this: from the trot, come back to walk for four or five strides, but all the while in the walk you keep thinking about the next trot, then ask for trot. Repeat this walk-trot transition in the same place on a big circle a few times, and see how the horse starts increasing his energy level for you.

• Make sure the horse's head is quite straight.

• Try using lighter and lighter seat, leg and stick aids, to make the horse listen harder.

• Ride the horse out with other horses that are lively company and learn the 'feel' of his body when he really moves out.

• Avoid a dull routine… try jumping, riding out and schooling on different days of the week to keep his mind fresh.

• Really shorten the paces and collect the horse as much as

Exercises like the shoulder-in can ultimately help a horse to go forwards brilliantly because, as you can see here with Arnie, they require him to take more athletic, stretching and deeper steps with his hind legs.

possible for a few strides – for example, in trot collect the horse by asking for something like the piaffe, which is trotting on the spot – then let him go forwards.

- Counter canter can induce more energy in the horse (see 'Wonderful Paces', page 112).
- Some horses learn to go forwards better on a looser rein, but some actually find that a little more contact in the reins helps them. Either way, make sure the contact stays consistent, so it doesn't 'come and go' in their mouth.

Jumping or riding over poles is a great way to give the horse variety in the arena. Jumping or polework can raise the horse's energy level and forwardness as he becomes more excited. The other advantage of this kind of work is its gymnastic value, as trotting or cantering over poles teaches the horse to use himself better.

One way to raise a slower horse's energy level is for him to be 'left behind' by his friends: here, Arnie is trotting with lots of impulsion to catch up with his friend!

WHEN THE HORSE GOES TOO FAST

With some horses, you can spend the whole time holding them back with the reins or your back: it is fun to start with, but soon becomes hard work and tiresome.

Many horses with a wonderful, forward-going attitude when ridden can easily turn that forward attitude into rushing, such as in this picture. When the horse rushes, he can use forward momentum to avoid collecting himself and using his muscles correctly. It is easy to think a very forward horse has good impulsion, but to me impulsion means the amount of energy asked for by the rider, rather than energy bursting out of the horse regardless of what the rider wants.

SOME TIPS TO GET LESS FORWARDNESS

- Firstly get the horse's teeth, tack and back checked to make sure he is not going too fast because of physical discomfort or pain.
- Ride small figures of eight or small circles (for example, 8m) in walk or trot. Stay passive, be patient, and wait for the horse to slow himself down. As much as possible, do nothing too active; instead of 'riding' the horse, sit on him and have the attitude that you are 'guiding' him and waiting.

- Do lots of work in walk: voltes (small circles), changes of direction and lateral movements. Walk for a long time at the beginning and end of your riding session, and at any other time the horse gets too forward or over-excited.
- Do lots of bends and turns, avoiding straight lines altogether, if possible.
- Try flexing the horse's neck a little to one side (see 'Soft Mouth', page 78).

Fantastique had become over-forward and excited outdoors, so I am riding small circles and changes of direction with loose reins and simply waiting for her to slow down.

Fantastique has lots of energy and impulsion but she can get ahead of me, as she has here, so I am flexing her head and beginning to turn her so as to steady the pace. Once she has steadied I will allow her to go straight again.

✓ DOs
- Pick a pattern that helps the horse to give you what you want: big patterns to go faster and small patterns to go more slowly.
- Make sure the horse is straight.
- Be really clear about your horse always going at the speed *you* choose.

✗ DON'Ts
- Don't resort to pulling on both reins to slow the horse down.
- Don't resort to kicking all the time in the hope of training the horse to be more forward-going.

Fantastique was rushing on her forehand down the straight side of the track, so I am asking her to turn a 10m circle to steady herself – although we may run over the photographer while doing so!

Fantastic Brakes

There is something wonderful about riding a horse with fantastic brakes: you can take him places, open up the throttle, go any speed you want and *know* he will stop when you ask him to with no questions. To my mind, the perfect riding horse should always stop with lightness when he is asked to, wherever he is and whatever pace he is moving at.

Have you ever sat on a horse and not been able to stop him? I have, and it can be an unpleasant and potentially dangerous experience for horse and rider. Culturally we seem to accept riding horses whose brakes are not reliable, but we wouldn't dream of driving a car in the same condition!

When you teach a horse to do good halts, you get more benefits than simply being able to stop him from moving: a good halt increases his suppleness, collection, and his gymnastic and elastic quality; it builds and stretches his muscles, and helps with his general level of attentiveness and obedience to the rider… And another advantage of knowing you can stop the horse any time, anywhere, is that it is great for your confidence level, which obviously affects how you ride and therefore how well the horse goes, too.

TWO DIFFERENT WAYS TO STOP

We are going to look at two quite different ways to stop: an emergency stop and a correct halt. Both of these methods need to be gradually trained into the horse and – when you take the time – both are useful pieces of the perfect riding horse jigsaw.

1. EMERGENCY STOP

If a horse has learned an emergency stop and you *know* you can always stop him whenever and wherever you want, you can relax much more with him in any situation. With an emergency stop, the great thing is that the horse *knows* you can stop him. Of course nothing is guaranteed in life, but with time and training you can get fairly close to 100 per cent reliability. With a bit of luck, you may never need to use this method of stopping, but it is useful to know it is there, just in case.

The idea of this method – which is for emergency use only – is that it is difficult for the horse to go anywhere when his head is flexed round to one side. It is a powerful move and should not be used to *force* or overpower the horse; rather, it works by putting him in an uncomfortable situation and waiting for him to sort himself out, and he usually does that by stopping.

This type of stop should be used without unbalancing the horse, so it is best to use it just as he starts to take off.

☐ HOW TO DO IT

1 From the ground and in the saddle, teach the horse to slowly flex his head softly and unquestioningly round to the right and left in the halt when you ask him with the rein (see 'Soft Mouth', page 78 to learn how to do this). This will prepare him nicely to yield when you ask.

2 Once he has learned to flex his head quietly round in the halt, ask him to walk on.

3 Next, think about stopping, cease moving your body with him and gently pick up one rein, slowly flexing his head around (picture A).

4 Keep him flexed, and then once he stops, release him and let him stand for a few moments (picture B).

IMPORTANT NOTE: If you grab or pick up the rein too sharply, the horse may react against it, rather than yielding softly to it.

5 Repeat steps 2 to 4 in different places in walk until it is second nature for both you and the horse. By now he should be stopping just when you *think* about picking up the rein, which means you may not have to actually flex his head.

6 Once the stop is established in walk, ask for the same thing from trot, but give him a little more time to respond to your request for him to flex, so he can change down the gears without losing his balance.

7 Once he stops when you *think* about picking up one rein in trot, ask for canter, and again give him even more time to flex than in walk or trot, as he needs to shift down the gears without losing his balance.

2. A CORRECT HALT

The ideal halt is one where you ride along in walk, trot or canter, think about stopping and the horse stops squarely, and in balance… exactly *where* you want, *when* you want, *how* you want, and without either of you pulling on the reins. He stops in the same outline and balance as he was while he was moving, with his hocks underneath him, and *you* don't have to do anything active, such as drawing back on the reins or stiffening your body.

Arnie is walking and listening well, and I am relaxed in my body and legs to flow with the movement of his walk.

How to do a Correct Halt

Many people ask me *how* to do a correct halt. It is really a matter of feel and timing with each individual horse, and if we become caught up in all the minute practical details of how to do it, we miss getting the feel and timing with the horse. I therefore recommend the exercise below, through which the horse will teach you his own personal feel and timing very quickly, then you can refine it by adding more impulsion to perfect it.

☐ HOW TO DO IT

1 Walk and allow yourself to flow with the horse's movement (picture A).
2 Pick a certain spot – for example a school letter, a tree, a fence post – and ask for a halt by *thinking* halt, and ceasing to flow with his movement (bring a little more tone into your spine); drop your legs and heels down a little, say 'whoa' if you have to, and cease *allowing* with the reins, so he 'walks' into them (picture B).
3 If the horse overshoots the spot you chose to halt at, notice by how many strides he does so. Do it again at another letter (only about 6 to 10 metres further on), and try letting him know you want to stop by thinking about it earlier… Now how many strides did he overshoot by?

I have decided to stop at letter E, and Arnie has already 'heard' my thought.

Do this three or four more times at different spots about 6 to 10 metres apart, adjusting your thought to halt, and with each successive halt reduce all your aids to a whisper (picture C).

4 If after five or six halts the horse is still not halting exactly where you want, ask him to rein back the exact number of strides by which he overshot the target spot (see 'Soft Mouth', page 78, for more on the reinback). Rest for a few moments at the spot where you wanted to halt, then repeat the exercise 10 metres further on, and continue...

5 When this is all going well in walk, repeat it in trot, and then in canter. And then pick places out of doors to repeat it, always checking your brakes as you go.

I asked Arnie in good time, and because he had a good purposeful walk, he has stopped just about square, too, although he is a little on his forehand.

Perry's Tip

If the horse *really* doesn't listen or stop at the place you asked for and pushes through your hands, or if he is getting tense, calmly put him on a very small circle – about 4 metres – using an open rein, and wait for him to stop (see 'Excellent Steering', page 68, for 'open rein'). When he does eventually stop, let him stand for a while and think how nice stopping is! Begin the halt exercise again, and repeat as necessary.

USING FLEXIONS

As we shall see in 'Smooth Transitions', page 102, it can sometimes be helpful to ask the horse for a little flexion of his head to the inside (one side or the other if he is not in an arena) before asking for a downward transition, in this case a transition down to halt. Having this flexion assists the horse in staying softer and maintaining his outline as he stops.

I am asking for a very gentle flexion to the inside, just enough to maintain Fantastique's softness prior to asking her to come back down to a walk and halt.

USING IMAGERY

I once had a pupil with a stunning dressage horse with so much power and 'go' in him it literally took 20 metres for his lady rider to stop him from a trot. I suggested a few things, but nothing worked very well. Then I remembered what she had first said to me, that this horse was the love of her life and meant the world to her… so I placed a couple of cones two metres apart, and dragged my heel to mark a line between the cones. I told her that the other side of the cones and the line was a 100-metre sheer cliff, and if the horse stepped over the line, she and the horse would fall to their deaths down the cliff; I then asked her to trot up as near to the edge as she dare.

The horse powered off round the arena – and stopped dead about half a metre from the edge. It was amazing. I asked her to repeat it, and it was the same every time: she could stop from trot in no strides, right near the edge. She did the same thing in canter with the same result. It showed me the horse could stop easily: what was needed was for the rider to be really committed. I have since used the image of the cones and the cliff many times with different horses and riders, and it really works.

Arnie is trotting well towards the 'cliff top', and my focus is very much on stopping as close to the line as possible.

Arnie has stopped better than I expected and with his foot right on the line… this is powerful stuff!

✓ DOs
- Educate the horse in easy stages, and that includes teaching him to have good brakes.
- Make sure you are really flowing with his movement when you are not asking him to stop, and then he will find it easier to notice the difference when you stop flowing to ask for a stop…it is the difference between flowing and not flowing that is ultimately the way to get great halts.

✗ DON'Ts
- Don't lean back (that can actually push him on, and put him on his forehand).
- Don't brace or lift your seat out of the saddle.
- Don't pull hard on both reins together: it makes horses pull even more strongly, push down on to the bridle, or poke their heads in the air.

Perfect Rider Checklist
- Train yourself not to pull both reins together, as the horse will probably pull on the reins in response, or he will throw his head up.
- Avoid grabbing the reins; you can do all your moves quickly but smoothly.

Excellent Steering

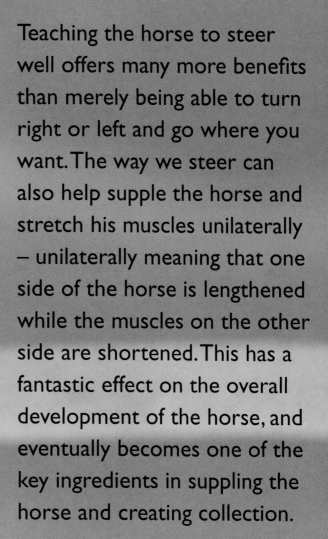

Teaching the horse to steer well offers many more benefits than merely being able to turn right or left and go where you want. The way we steer can also help supple the horse and stretch his muscles unilaterally – unilaterally meaning that one side of the horse is lengthened while the muscles on the other side are shortened. This has a fantastic effect on the overall development of the horse, and eventually becomes one of the key ingredients in suppling the horse and creating collection.

The aim of good steering is that the rider thinks about turning at a precise spot, and then horse and rider turn together as one creature, with no discernible aids. As a result of the turn, the horse's hindquarters are more engaged under his body and his carriage improves.

Steering and guiding the horse well also has the benefit of increasing his attentiveness, as well as teaching him to listen and relax.

STEERING EFFECTIVELY

When we steer a horse correctly, we don't just use the reins: we use our whole self. Because we humans do most things with our hands, it is easy to focus or rely too much on the hands in order to ask horses to turn; but the reins are only a part of the story. What should happen when we steer a horse is that we turn ourselves as one piece: that means our head, body, legs and hands all turn together, the same amount at the same time... and the horse turns himself underneath us.

Also, being human, we tend to think about things too much, make things complicated, and try too hard to get results. But where steering horses is concerned, the answer is nearly always 'less is more'. Turning the horse should be as effortless as if we were simply turning ourselves without the horse underneath us.

Probably the most important element in turning the horse is not the reins, our legs or body, but our focus or intention.

When we are really clear about where we want to go, and let the horse know in plenty of time, quite often that is all we need to do: the physical aids become almost non-existent, even on a young horse. The reason for this is that horses in the herd communicate a lot with each other using focus. When the herd leader lifts her head up from grazing and looks at something, the rest of the herd tends to focus on the same thing, and when the herd leader moves towards something she is focusing on, the rest of the herd tends to follow. So the most essential part of effective steering is having a clear focus and commitment about where we want to go.

If the basic task of getting the horse to go where we want to go is taken care of mostly with focus and intention, it frees up our legs, body and rein aids to be more refined. The aids then contribute to more than just turning: they help bring about better carriage, lightness and collection from the horse through the turns.

In this photo you can see very clearly how a light inside leg and supporting outside rein does more than steer the horse round to the right: Fantastique has raised her forehand and collected through her frame as a result of turning in this way.

USING THE LEGS WHEN TURNING

Many people talk about 'using the inside leg to turn', but what does this actually mean? The most useful way to use the inside leg is not to press it on the horse or to draw it inwards, but to think of taking a step down a stair with the inside foot, which means you release the leg all the way from the hip. This makes it easier for the horse to bend round the leg and move through the turn.

The outside leg will help to guide the outside of the horse in a nice passive way if it naturally follows the turn being made by you and the horse.

Although my inside leg is still in light contact with Fantastique's side, I have clearly released it to invite her to turn round it. She is a little heavy on her front, and that could be because I am focusing down too much as we turn, and also because I am not asking for enough impulsion or lift from her hindquarters.

Perfect Rider Checklist

Good steering ultimately involves both reins and the rider's body and legs... the rider's body and legs should turn as if without the horse. The result is that the outside leg and rein play important roles in guiding the horse, albeit in a 'passive' way – that is, not *doing* anything actively. When the rider stays in balance and remains upright from tip to toe, it helps the horse to stay in balance... It is not necessary for the rider to twist their head or their waist, or to drop their weight down one side of the saddle or the other: these things get in the horse's way and make it more difficult for him to turn gracefully and easily.

FOUR WAYS TO USE THE REINS TO STEER

Because of the way our human minds work, it can be quite difficult to get out of the habit of steering by pulling the right rein to go right and the left rein to go left... unfortunately, this is not the correct way to steer a horse.

We will assume that the rider's body and legs are turning with the horse, and what I now want to do is explain four ways the rider can use the reins, which will lead to good steering in a step-by-step way.

1. OPEN REIN

In the open rein, the rider's hand is taken out to the side, away from the neck. The hand should not be drawn backwards but simply out to the side, creating an almost irresistible, and yet passive, invitation for the horse to turn. The great thing about the open rein is that, if a horse is good to lead, you don't have to really teach it; the horse just follows the feel of the open rein and steps into the space created by the rein being opened away from the neck.

The open rein is good for young horses, for relaxing tense horses, and for a natural way of stretching the horse's muscles in his neck and body.

This picture shows an open rein from above. The degree to which you take the hand away from the neck is dependent upon the result you are getting. Ideally the rein opens only a little away from the neck, but it is perfectly all right to take it out further and further from the neck if necessary.

This photo shows the effect of an open rein steering the horse. Notice how it passively invites the horse to turn his front end, which lowers and relaxes his neck and head.

Useful patterns to ride for improving steering

Small circles at every letter in the arena

Figures of eight

Snake-type patterns

Squares

2. DIRECT REIN

The most common way that we see horses being turned is not with an open rein, but with some variation or other on the 'direct rein' – pulling the right rein to go right, and the left rein to go left. Some people might class the direct rein as the same as the open rein, but to me, the direct rein stays near to the horse's neck.

Despite its pitfalls, using the direct rein very subtly, and combining it with the support of the outside rein (as we shall see in the fourth method, see over) gives us a very good turn indeed, so it is worth teaching the horse this aid, which you might like to think of as a minimized open rein.

This way of steering (the right rein to go right and the left rein to go left) suits our human mind's way of thinking about steering, but sometimes all this rein aid does is turn the horse's head and not his body… so you might end up with his head to the right, but the horse actually going off to the left, for example.

A direct rein shown from above. It acts mostly on the horse's head, which is not really ideal for turning the whole horse, but is useful if you want to turn the horse's head or to ask him for a flexion of the head to one side.

Here is the result of the direct rein steering the horse. You can see it turns his head more than it turns the rest of him, and can cause him to fall on to his outside shoulder, which unbalances him.

3. NECK REIN

The neck rein is best known in Western riding and is normally performed with loose reins. To neck rein, the rider usually has both reins in one hand, guiding the horse to go left or right by moving the hand across to the left or right to indicate the required direction. In effect, the neck rein simultaneously opens one rein, whilst the other rein comes against the horse's neck and moves him away from it.

Teaching horses to neck rein is a useful stage for making them 'handy' and relaxed. Neck reining is good to use outdoors, and can also be helpful as a stage towards teaching the horse the correct way to turn (see the fourth method,

opposite) with support from the outside rein. I want to be able to ride my horses, especially outdoors, without a constant feel on their mouth, so neck reining is a useful skill for the horse to understand.

To teach neck reining takes longer with some horses than others: horses that are sensitive to touch or light on their feet move away from the neck rein very easily. Less sensitive horses can be slower to learn this aid, so you may have to spend time teaching them to yield away from a touch on their neck from the ground first (see 'Yielding the forehand', page 96).

The neck rein shown from above. Although it is possible to perform this aid with the reins held in both hands, the rider usually holds both reins in one hand.

This is the effect of a neck rein on turning the horse. Notice how it is bringing his shoulders and forelegs across, so he is effectively turning with his forehand, rather than just his head.

4. TURNING WITH BOTH REINS TOGETHER

Turning with both reins is what I think of as the correct way to turn, and it has a number of advantages over the other methods. The most difficult thing about turning with both reins is that our human mind finds the concept of the outside rein being at least as important as the inside rein very challenging to accept.

As a result of steering with both reins together, the inside rein naturally asks for a tiny bit of bend in the horse's head and opens slightly away from his neck.

The outside rein comes in towards the horse's outside shoulder and neck, and supports his outside shoulder: because it does this, the horse is likely to make the turn in a more 'whole' way, with his body, neck and head all following the same arc, as though he turns in one piece.

Simply by turning in this way, the horse is invited to collect and use himself in a favourable manner, engaging his hind legs so that his pushing power goes from his hindquarters right up through his body to his poll.

You can see from this picture that to perform a nice turn using both reins requires the hands to do very little. This keeps the horse in 'one piece' and turns the whole of him quite successfully, with far less likelihood of creating problems such as having him 'fall out' on the circle. Try this approach and see just how little you need to do to ask the horse to turn – it may well be even less than you see in this photo.

It is quite clear from this picture how using both reins to turn the horse helps him to maintain a nice shape and to turn in 'one piece', where his body follows easily on the curving line made by the direction his head is pointing.

PRACTISING STEERING OUTDOORS

Riding out gives you lots of opportunities to use natural features for steering practice, and is also a good way to get your horse listening to you more.

Steering Fantastique through this maze of silver birch trees using both reins and a light inside leg increased her engagement and helped to improve her carriage, too. I did this for about five minutes, changing direction round the trees all the time. At first she wondered what I was doing, then she became interested, the steering aids became lighter and lighter, and her body really softened and suppled up.

Perry's Tips

With Fantastique's invaluable help, here are examples of incorrect and correct ways to turn the horse:

The wrong way to turn: many of us are told to *use* the inside leg to turn, which results in the leg being drawn up or inwards in all manner of strange and unsuccessful ways. Perhaps because we learn to ride bicycles before we learn to ride horses, we tend to rely on the inside rein to ask horses to turn, as in this picture!

The right way to turn: with the hands staying in the same position relative to my body, *I simply turn.* When this is done on the horse, 99 times out of 100 it is enough to turn the horse and helps him to remain in balance under you, because you are both turning together as one whole six-legged creature.

✓ DOs

- Step lightly down into your inside foot.
- Know exactly where you are going.
- Focus your mind where you want to go, but always be gazing between the horse's ears.
- Keep it simple and clear.

✗ DON'Ts

- Don't turn your head or twist your upper body to turn the horse.
- Don't press your inside leg against the horse (horses are 'into-pressure' creatures, and they will press back against you).
- Don't tip your weight to one side or the other.

Soft Mouth

A horse with a nice soft mouth can be a real pleasure to ride: he balances himself underneath you without leaning on the bit, he listens and responds to small 'feels' in your hands, and there is a real communication going on between the two of you through the reins. A horse with a hard mouth is quite different, and can be unpleasant and hard work.

The good news is, it is possible to teach most horses to have a nice mouth, and even many so-called 'hard-mouthed' horses can be softened up with some success.

Rein contact is the first thing some people think about when we talk about a horse's mouth, but it is only a part of developing a 'soft mouth'; it is also important to develop his softness and responsiveness to the rider's leg, as well as the overall suppleness in his body so he collects easily, stepping well underneath himself with his hindquarters.

Just like us, the horse's mind and body are intrinsically linked, which means we also need to work on him being 'accepting' and 'soft' in his mind, so he can be 'accepting' and 'soft' in his mouth (see 'A Great Partner' and 'Listens to the Rider', pages 26 and 36).

We will begin by teaching the horse exercises to develop a soft mouth in hand (from the ground). If either you or the horse are not clear about the exercises, it is a good plan to start in a halter and then, when you both have the idea, to repeat them in a snaffle bit.

SIMPLE STEPS TO SUCCESSFUL IN-HAND WORK

During the next few chapters we will be using 'in-hand' work to introduce the horse to various exercises or to improve his responsiveness, before trying the exercises under the rider. By the term 'in hand' I mean working closely alongside the horse, using a halter or a bridle, and using your hand or stick to do the job your legs will do when riding.

- In-hand work is a wonderful way to show the horse what you want, and it prepares him both physically and mentally to be ridden.
- This approach warms up his body without the weight of a rider, and helps you to see and feel how he is moving, and where he is stiff, before you get on him.
- As with everything you do around horses, in-hand work should be done in a very calm and slow way, especially while you both become accustomed to it; remember that horses can easily become confused or upset if they don't understand what is required.

- Always reward him and let him know when he is doing right.
- Once you and the horse have learned some of the in-hand exercises in this book, you will find it of huge benefit to spend even just five minutes every day doing some of the exercises as a preparation before you ride, whether you are schooling, competing or simply going for a pleasurable hack in the countryside.

EXERCISE 1
FLEXING THE NECK FROM THE GROUND

For a horse to be responsive and soft in his mouth, it is important that he is soft in his neck. A horse with a supple neck is likely to be easier to bring on to the bit, as well as being easier to guide and control. Many horses who are strong on the reins are not actually hard in the mouth, but are braced or stiff in their neck; so the first way to approach softness is to flex the horse's neck. This can be especially the case with thick-set horses and ponies with short, deep necks relative to their overall conformation.

NOTE: Flexing the neck should be done gently and with discretion, and should be developed over many months: we do not want to force the horse, nor create a horse with a 'floppy' neck; we are doing this to have him nicely supple and relaxed, so that when we ask something with the rein, he happily says 'Yes, I can do this,' rather than 'No, I can't do that because I am braced against you with my neck.'

HOW TO DO IT

1. Stand the horse fairly square and position yourself near his shoulder, about an arm's length from him. Gently pick up the rein nearest to you, and ask him to yield his head round. 'Invite' his head, rather than pulling it. Be very light, and wait for the horse's response.
2. When his head comes round and you feel him soften the contact, release him by letting go of the rein and letting him put his head straightaway
3. If the horse moves his feet when you ask him for the flexion of his neck, he is probably showing you he is stiff somewhere in his body – probably his hindquarters or neck; this means the exercise is worth practising regularly until he can perform it without moving them.
4. If he does move his feet, try to quietly move with him, maintaining your request for flexion; or repeat the exercise a few more times and try approaching it a little more slowly and softly. Body language and position are also important, so try standing in a slightly different place in relation to the horse, to see if it helps him to understand that you don't want him to move his feet, just yield his head to you.
5. Make sure you do the exercise from both sides, and notice which side he is stiffer on.
6. Once the horse has learned to flex his neck nicely in the halter, repeat it with his bridle and bit on. It is a good idea to ask for a flexion from both sides a couple of times each day before you ride.

EXERCISE 2
FLEXING THE NECK FROM THE SADDLE

Once the horse has become accustomed to yielding his head from the ground, it is time to ask the same thing from the saddle. Remember to ask him very gently and slowly, as we don't want him to move his feet, just yield his head round. The ultimate aim is to teach the horse to flex his head round in response to the rider's leg, which means when you put your left leg on, the horse brings his head round to the left, and when you put your right leg on the horse brings his head round to the right. So when you ride the horse on a circle, for example, having your inside leg on means that the horse bends to the inside in response to your leg, rather than just to the inside rein; and if you ride a straight line with *both* legs lightly on, the horse bends longitudinally (that is, he drops his nose and comes on to the bit) from the feel of your legs and not just from the reins.

HOW TO DO IT

1. Bring the horse to a good halt and then let him relax there for a few moments.
2. Let your legs hang totally passively on his sides, then gently apply one leg at the girth and softly pick up one rein (on the same side as your applied leg). Open the rein slightly away from the horse's neck and curve it round towards your hip, making sure you also ease the other rein out so it doesn't restrict his head coming round.
3. If the horse flexes his head round and softens without moving his feet, wait three or four seconds, then release your leg and let go of the rein so he can straighten his head.
4. If the horse can't flex his head without moving his feet, keep your legs and seat quiet, and passively hold the rein so he moves on a tiny circle until he finds his balance, stands still and yields his neck to you. This should all be done very calmly. When he finally stops and yields, hold for three or four seconds, then release him.

5. Ultimately, when the horse feels a soft leg on his side, he should flex his head slightly round to that side, even before you pick up the rein; this will help you in gaining soft self-carriage at a later stage.

Once the horse has learned to flex nicely in halt, try it in walk and eventually trot. It helps to ask for the flexion as you ride along a straight line – such as the long side of the arena – so you have a guide and can keep his body straight whilst asking for a soft yield. I ask the horse to flex his head to the 'outside' on one long side of the arena, then flex it to the 'inside' on the next long side… that way he is being worked evenly on both sides of his neck and I can feel on which side he is a little stiff.

Perry's Tips

People sometimes say their horse can bring his head round easily for a titbit, but not from a feel on the reins, and ask me if that is all right. However, looking for a titbit does not have the same benefit because it is not teaching the horse to yield in response to the reins, which is what we are doing in Exercises 1 and 2.

EXERCISE 3
REINBACK FROM THE GROUND AND THE SADDLE...

Showing the position for asking the horse to reinback from the ground. Make sure you use a light feel on the reins, rather than a hard pull.

The reinback from the ground (in hand) is a good way to have a conversation with your horse's mouth, and can really teach him about yielding softly to both reins. For the purpose of this exercise we generally ask for just two or three steps of reinback each time to begin with.

In the reinback the horse should step steadily and rhythmically backwards in a straight line. His feet should move in diagonal pairs, the same as in the trot (left foreleg and right hind leg, then right foreleg and left hind leg).

Reinback is a useful exercise for suppling the horse through his back and for softening the contact with the bit. It can also be used to collect the horse and to put him more on to his hindquarters.

It is also useful in many practical applications, for example opening and closing gates.

HOW TO DO IT

1. Stand just to one side of your horse's head and lightly take up both reins, one in each hand, about four or five inches from his mouth. (You could begin in a halter and rope until the horse understands the exercise, and then use a bit... I do this with all of my horses.)
2. Move the reins back gently and wait for the horse to respond, which he will do either by mouthing and 'talking' a little on the bit, or by taking a step backwards.
3. As the horse yields to the request on the rein, lighten your hands a little as a reward.
4. Repeat steps 2 and 3 for each new step of reinback. Use *both reins the same,* but put your *attention* on the rein that matches the horse's foremost foreleg – that is, the one he is about to move next. This lets him know you are really in tune with him, and lightens his response to the aid.
5. If the horse's hindquarters waver off to one side when you ask for reinback, first ask him when he is adjacent to a fence. Ultimately you want to correct his wavering hindquarters by shifting his forehand across so it is in front of his hindquarters; this will help him to strengthen up and collect (see 'Light, Responsive and Obedient to the Aids', page 92, to find out how).

Once the horse has learned to yield to both reins and to rein back softly in hand, ask him to rein back from the saddle.

Hold the reins lightly and invite the horse to step backwards, softening your hands the instant he responds.

...AND UNDER SADDLE

Take it steady and do one step at a time, softening the rein contact a little each time he steps back. Make sure you ask politely with the reins and wait for him to take a step back, rather than pulling hard on him. If you need to pull hard on the reins for reinback from the saddle, I would suggest doing more work on the reinback in hand until it is nice and soft, before trying under saddle.

Some people use a lot of leg in the reinback from the saddle, or tip their bodies too far forwards or backwards. Any of these aids can confuse the horse and lose the flow of the reinback. If you have taught the horse from the ground first, and then you ask politely and with quiet aids from the saddle, most horses – even young ones – will perform reinback with no problem. You can then use a little leg for extra collection or 'lift'.

Some more useful exercises to help gain softness in the mouth:

- Ride circles and turns rather than straight lines.
- Ask for *lots* of transitions on a big circle.
- Practise riding lateral work, especially movements such as shoulder-in on a circle (see 'Dances the Lateral Movements', page 122, to find out how).

USING THE LEGS AND STICK FOR A SOFT MOUTH

For the horse to be soft in the mouth, not only does he need to respond well to the reins, he also needs to 'come up from behind' and respond to the rider's leg or stick by going forwards.

It is by bringing his hindquarters forwards underneath him that the horse shortens his whole frame, arches his back and neck, and becomes truly soft in the mouth. It is therefore really important to teach the horse to respond to very light leg aids (see 'Calm, Willing and Forward-going', page 50). Another tip which can also be useful for asking the horse to be softer in his mouth is to literally touch him on the hindquarters with the end of the stick. You may even try resting the end of the stick lightly on his side for a couple of strides to see if it helps him soften to the bridle. It is important to use the stick so lightly that it does not surprise him or make him speed up, which would probably make him push forwards more into the bridle, rather than rounding himself and softening the rein contact.

Arnie is not being soft on the bridle in this picture because he is not really working forwards with his back legs.

I have used my legs and touched him lightly with the stick to ask him to step up more from behind and into the bridle. This has made him softer, not only in his mouth but through his whole body.

Learning to relax

It is not a good idea to ride the horse on the bit all the time: it is really essential that he learns to go on a long, loose rein to relax in his mind and his body. I want the horse to be happy, whether he is in the school or outdoors, on a loose rein.

BITS AND BRIDLES

TRAINING IN A HACKAMORE OR HALTER

To use a hackamore, halter, bosal or cavesson to begin with is traditional in Western and classical training, and helps to keep the mouth soft.

For many years I have 'started' young horses in a hackamore, bitless bridle or halter, because it gives them the chance to learn the basics of being a riding horse whilst preserving the softness of the mouth. Assuming you have taught the horse to lead very well in a halter he should be quite responsive in the hackamore. Riding without a bit is a good way to keep things simple and uncomplicated for the young horse, which may become confused, worried or uncomfortable by the action of the bit.

Although the bosal or cavesson is the traditional equipment, I find it more practical to use a simple rope halter for this stage of training (see pictures overleaf).

NOTE: Only ride in a rope halter or hackamore in a safe situation, such as in an arena, and only if the horse is controllable and responsive in this equipment.

A traditional Western bosal. Training the young or spoiled horse without a bit can help to create a soft mouth when the bit is introduced or reintroduced.

HOW TO USE A HACKAMORE:

- Aim to keep some slack in the reins (see pictures below).
- To turn left, open the left rein out to the left; and to turn right, open the right rein out to the right.
- To stop or rein back, keep one rein still and bring the other rein back towards your hip, giving and taking the contact a little.

- To emergency stop, bend him as described in the chapter 'Fantastic Brakes' (see page 62).
- To ask him to drop his nose into an outline, keep one rein still and 'feel' or vibrate the other rein a little.

Once the horse is well established in walk, trot and canter, and when he turns, stops, yields to the leg and reins back in the halter, I will gradually introduce him to the jointed snaffle bit.

Use an open rein to turn in the hackamore or bitless bridle.

Light vibrations of one rein ask the horse to drop his nose and relax his neck.

The hackamore or bitless bridle should be used without a constant contact.

TRAINING IN THE SNAFFLE

For a time I ride young horses with two sets of reins, one on the halter and one on the snaffle, so I can use the snaffle lightly when he is listening to me, and the halter for firmer control if necessary, without touching his mouth. The snaffle is a very useful bit for schooling horses because it has a joint in the middle and therefore you can use it to work with – and talk to – one side of the horse at a time, for example flexing or bending down one side.

Unlike other bits or variations of bits, the simple jointed snaffle also has the added advantage (though it may not seem so at the time!) that it doesn't hide or mask anything that is going on with the horse in his training or his way of going. So the snaffle doesn't make things easier, but it shows us very clearly what areas of the horse need working on.

I use a simple eggbutt snaffle because it gives the most 'honest picture' of what is going on throughout the horse's body when he is being ridden.

TRAINING IN THE DOUBLE BRIDLE AND CURB

When the horse is further on in his training I like to use the double bridle, which needs the horse to be well established in his work and responsive to the seat and legs, and the rider to have an independent seat and light hands. The double bridle – which has two bits, the snaffle and the curb – is a fantastic tool, and helps develop more finesse and subtlety into the aids; however, it is not very easy to use correctly and requires some experience. The snaffle part of the double bridle can be used to 'talk' independently to one side of the horse or the other, and the curb rein is introduced to refine the communication between horse and rider.

The double bridle offers a wide array of possibilities, as the snaffle can be used to raise the front of the horse, and the curb asks for more flexion at the poll and can also be used to entice the horse to reach forwards with his neck.

Riding with the curb bit alone (which also makes up part of the double bridle) requires the rider to be able to adapt their riding and to lighten the use of the reins to suit this more severe bit. The horse should be at the stage where he is very settled in his carriage and will bend and turn from the rider's leg and seat alone, without relying on the reins to steer him. Ideally, by the time the horse is in a curb, it is possible to ride him one-handed, without a constant contact, and most of the communication between horse and rider is through subtle body messages (see pictures on page 90).

Perry's Bridle Tips

- Different horses have differently shaped mouths, so it is important that you use a bit or bridle the horse is comfortable with.
- Much time is normally spent in training using the snaffle bit.
- It is important to understand that whatever bit you use, it is only as good or bad as the rider's hands on the other end of the reins.
- The rider needs to adapt their use of the reins depending on the type of bridle being used.

There are a number of ways to hold the reins of the double bridle, but the most common way is with the snaffle rein in the usual place between the ring finger and the little finger, and the curb rein between the index finger and the second finger.

The double bridle is a fantastic piece of tack when used with finesse. Both horse and rider need to be well settled in their work before introducing what could be a severe arrangement in the wrong hands.

Riding a half-pass in the curb bit: you can see how the horse is responding by bending to my leg and being guided by my seat. This is important with the curb bit, because, unlike the snaffle, this bit doesn't have a link, it is one straight bar in the mouth rather than in two halves. The curb bridle is kept very light and very quiet in the hand, so the horse feels totally at ease and trusting of his rider.

Here I am cantering Fantastique in a curb bit. Even in the faster paces, the curb bit should be kept quite light with the contact slightly loose. In order for the rider's hands to be absolutely still, and so as to avoid catching the horse in the mouth with the bit, it is important to learn to absorb the horse's movement through your seat, especially in the trot and canter.

A WORD OF WARNING

It can be very tempting to go out and acquire a more severe bit in order to get a horse to feel softer in the mouth or more controllable, but usually this only masks the symptoms, rather than dealing with the causes of why the horse may be strong. If a horse is strong, it is usually a sign that he needs more time spent schooling or re-schooling his whole body in order to help him be more supple and yielding.

Perfect Rider Checklist

To get the horse's mouth soft under saddle, try turning your hands upright (thumbs on top), with your wrists soft and straight, fingers closed on the rein, and the upper body upright and balanced – avoid leaning back. Relax the small of your back and buttocks, and think of riding with your elbows, rather than your hands. Have your heels gently lowered (or the toes raised).

After a touch of your legs on the horse's sides, try the lightest touch of the stick behind your leg, *not to go any faster*, but to invite the horse to 'come up into the bridle'.

✓ DOs

- Look for moments of 'soft feel'.
- Give the horse time to say 'yes' to you.
- Ask, and then wait for a response.
- 'Release' the moment the horse 'releases'.
- Always begin each request incredibly lightly.
- Pay attention to the whole horse working through his body from the hindquarters, not just his mouth or the position of his head. A horse with a very soft mouth, or a rider with hard hands, can cause the horse to be behind the bit or just have his head pulled into position, which is not what we want him to do.

✗ DON'Ts

- Don't pull hard, yank or begin any rein aids suddenly or strongly.
- Don't overdo flexing exercises (just a couple of times each side per day should be enough).

Light, Responsive and Obedient to the Aids

Whatever your style of riding or chosen equestrian discipline, it makes the world of difference to your level of performance and enjoyment if the horse is light, responsive and obedient to the aids. When a horse is responsive, he happily and immediately does what you are asking of him with ease and softness.

The question is, *how* do we get a horse to be that way? Actually, everything in this book is a part of the answer, but one of the most important things is to train the horse to be supple. A supple horse is generally calm, obedient and a real pleasure to ride because he finds it easy to do what you ask without 'bracing' against you.

An added benefit of teaching the horse to be supple and responsive is that he also becomes easier to manoeuvre and therefore – in theory – a safer horse to ride and control.

Assuming you have already done the exercises in the previous chapter ('Soft Mouth'), your horse should be getting lighter on the reins and more responsive to the leg aids. In this chapter we are going to add the next few pieces of the jigsaw and really get the horse responsive and 'tuned up' to the aids. With this training, you should also find your partnership with the horse naturally developing on a deeper and more rewarding level.

For the best results, we are again going to use in-hand work first, in order to teach the horse what is required, and to help him to be more responsive. We will then repeat each exercise under saddle.

EXERCISE 1
YIELDING THE HINDQUARTERS (TURN ON THE FOREHAND)

A good riding horse needs to be supple in his hindquarters and obedient to the leg aids. This exercise helps him become supple in the hips, and teaches him to move away from the rider's leg. It can also make the horse more responsive and forward off the leg.

HOW TO DO IT

1. Stand near the horse's shoulder with one hand holding the rein about four inches from the bit, and the other hand placed about four inches behind the girth, holding the stick near his hindquarters.

2. Use your 'rein hand' to ask him to flex his head slightly towards you, and place your 'stick hand' on his side just behind the girth, touching him very lightly in the place where your leg will be when you ride.

3. If he responds by yielding his hindquarters sideways one step, relax and reward him by relaxing your stick hand. (The hind leg nearest you should cross in front of the other hind leg.)

4. If the horse doesn't respond to the light feel of your hand behind the girth, keep the hand in place and support it by touching him rhythmically on his quarters with the stick until he yields. As soon as he responds, reward him by 'releasing'.

5. After one good step, pause, relax, stroke the horse, then ask for another step. Look for one quality step at a time, rather than have him rush the steps.

6. Repeat the exercise on the other side.

7. Finally, perform it again under saddle, replacing your 'stick hand' on his side with your leg.

THREE THINGS TO REMEMBER

1. Every time you use an aid to ask for something, start asking very lightly and gradually increase or repeat the aid more strongly until the horse responds.

2. To teach a horse to be light, as soon as he responds to our aid or request, we instantly lighten our contact or release him from the aid.

3. With every exercise, always practise the same thing on both sides of the horse.

I am asking Fantastique to yield her right hindquarter away from my right leg, which is placed just behind the girth. Notice how I have a very slight bend of her head to the right. I am keeping my weight quite central so I don't disturb her balance and cause her to do more than simply yield her right hind leg.

EXERCISE 2
YIELDING THE FOREHAND

We need to teach the horse to be willing to move his front end round his back end. Yielding the forehand helps with manoeuvrability and lightens his forehand, which will ultimately help him to engage his hindquarters and collect himself.

HOW TO DO IT

1. Stand just in front of his shoulder with your body turned towards him, and apply gentle pressure to his neck with one hand and the lower part of his shoulder with the other (picture A). Think of stepping forwards into him as you ask. (The exact place to stand and touch varies slightly on each horse, so you need to experiment.) This movement can the horse take time to learn, so be patient and look for one good step (picture B).

I am using finger-tip pressure to ask **Arnie** to move his forehand away from me. I gradually increase the finger-tip pressure until he responds, but I do not by any means get into a pushing match with him: he weighs 650kg, so it would be a waste of time! Instead, I am using the power of my intention and the body energy from my solar plexus (stomach) to support my fingers' request for him to move his forehand away from me.

2. Once he understands to step his front away from you, pick up the reins. As in picture C (with both hands in the same area as before), ask the horse to turn his head a little away from you and have him yield his front again, but this time have some of your attention on the reins. Apply the same gentle pressure on his neck and shoulder, and use the reins to support it.

3. Once the horse performs the movement easily and lightly from the ground, ask him from the saddle (pictures C and D).

Having learned to yield his forehand from the ground, Arnie demonstrates yielding his forehand round his haunches quite easily under saddle. Note how it is not done by pulling the horse round with the reins, or by crossing the reins over the withers. It is important when asking the horse to do this movement that you do each step slowly to give him time to readjust his balance, otherwise he whips round quickly and his hindquarters swing out, which is not what we want.

CIRCLES AND VOLTES (SMALL CIRCLES)

Riding circles is one of the cornerstones of most forms of education for the riding horse. To create the perfect riding horse, circles are incredibly useful. Circles help to engage the horse's inside hind leg and increase his suppleness and strength. They also flex his muscles and stretch the outside of his neck and body, which helps make it easier to ask him for a good 'outline'. Circles are also helpful in retaining the horse's mental focus – that is, giving him and us a simple and clear pattern or framework within which to have a conversation.

Riding circles without thinking about what they look like or how they feel can be very boring for the horse and rider; but circles done well are an important tool in creating the perfect riding horse, and can be interesting for both partners.

You can see how riding on the circle is helping Fantastique to round her carriage by stepping well under her body with the inside hind leg.

TIPS ON CIRCLES

- Make sure the circle is really accurate and ends exactly where it began: horses try to change the shape of the circle to avoid using themselves very well.
- If the horse cuts in repeatedly on the circle, try riding a big square first (just four straight lines!). When the square is really established, gradually round off the corners, and there's your circle!
- Balance your weight over the horse's centre, not tipping in or out.
- When riding circles, step down a little with your inside foot by releasing your leg from the hip.
- Keep a feel on both reins: the outside rein is at least as important as the inside rein (see 'Excellent Steering', page 68). If at all possible, avoid using the inside rein more than the outside rein in order to turn the horse, as this turns his head more than his body and you then lose the quality of the horse's shape.
- Do as many circles on the right rein as the left, and notice how the horse is different on each rein… probably softer on one side and stiffer on the other (most horses feel 'softer' on the right). Our aim is to work with him to make the circles more even on both sides, by straightening him up a little on the soft side and bending him a little more on the stiff side.
- Ask the horse to look a little into the circle with his head using your inside rein and leg.
- Watch for the horse 'falling out' and putting more weight on to his outside shoulder: if he does this you probably need to support him with a little more outside rein and leg, and have his head bent *less* into the inside of the circle.
- You can ride 20m, 10m, 8m or 6m circles, according to the horse's level of training and what you require… the smaller the circle, the more engagement and collection you will get from the horse. Small circles are hard work for the horse, so make sure you don't overdo them – and remember that small circles can decrease the speed and impulsion of the horse. Big circles have the advantage of creating a nice bend in the horse whilst preserving the forwardness and impulsion.

Even though riding out is generally a time to allow the horse to relax, it doesn't mean we can't ask him for a circle now and then. Riding the occasional circle outdoors keeps the horse listening, and helps to soften and rebalance him, too.

SPIRALS

Spirals are a good way to reap the benefits of both big and small circles all in one exercise, improving the horse's outline and bend whilst maintaining forward movement. Spirals also teach the horse to listen more carefully to our aids (especially the outside rein and leg), since we are changing the size of the pattern all the time.

In walk, trot or canter, start riding a 20m circle. Then by 'feeling' the outside rein a little, gradually decrease the size of the circle to as small as you can (perhaps even down to about 6m) without losing the gait or the rhythm. Then spiral back out to 20m again, asking the horse to move outwards by confirming – not squeezing or pressing – your inside leg.

✓ DOs
- Notice which parts of the horse are braced or blocking the flow of movement, and then notice where your body may be doing the same (often horses and riders mirror each other's stiffness).
- Enjoy the process of suppling and training the horse towards perfection.
- Start your daily rides with five minutes or so of in-hand exercises.

✗ DON'Ts
- Don't be in a hurry.
- Don't think the horse is being difficult: probably he doesn't understand the request, or he is too stiff to do it easily.

SQUARES

It is common to see people riding circles these days, but horses are not often ridden on squares. In days gone by, training horses by riding squares for the purpose of their athletic training was much more usual.

There are some useful benefits to riding squares, not least that it keeps the horse guessing. One moment he is on a straight line, the next he is asked to turn through a 90-degree corner, then another straight line. Unlike the circle, where the horse can settle his body into a particular bend and more or less stay like that until we change the rein, on a square the horse is asked to straighten, then bend, then straighten again, then bend. The other advantage of squares is that, because the corners are naturally very tight, he has to really collect himself for a moment to turn.

Fantastique in the centre of a spiral: notice how riding this pattern is engaging her hindquarters.

Smooth Transitions

Technically speaking, a transition is when the horse goes up or down from one gait (walk, trot or canter) to another. But in reality, transitions are more than just a way of changing gear or speed, they are an opportunity to rebalance and collect the horse. They can also improve responsiveness, increase elasticity, lightness and 'spring', and help to gain more of the horse's attention.

Practising good transitions is not necessarily easy for the rider and can be quite demanding on the horse too, but they are an invaluable part of creating the perfect riding horse. The reason transitions are so beneficial is that, when going up or down from one gait to another, the horse has to momentarily place his hindquarters a little further underneath his body and use the power in his muscles to tighten and then release him into the next gait. This means he becomes stronger and more collected as a result.

Transitions should ultimately be 'on the button', which means they happen exactly when the rider asks for them, but just as importantly, the horse should maintain the quality of his carriage throughout the transition.

DOWNWARD TRANSITIONS

- Teach the horse to listen to small body cues by flowing with him before you ask for a downward transition, then flow less with him to change down.
- Know specifically what you want after the transition, with your mind and body, so the horse listens and gives what you want, rather than him simply 'falling' out of the gait you are in. When coming down from trot to walk, for example, think of going forwards into a walk.
- Use either a curve or a circle to soften the downward transition (you can also use this technique on the upward transition).
- Avoid the horse leaning on your reins for a downward transition, by not relying solely on the reins to acheive the transition.
- Be sure to pick a specific place to change down: this is really important.

The horse is trotting well, and I begin thinking about a downward transition to the walk.

Still in trot; notice how Fantastique's body shortens and collects to prepare for the walk.

Perry's Tips

- 'Feel' the horse for a good moment to ask for your transition.
- Working on a 20m circle, do lots of transitions, perhaps four per circle, and in and out of all the gaits; include halt and reinback, too.
- Try breathing out as you ask for upward or downward transitions.
- Flex the horse's head a tiny bit before transitions to make them smoother or to help him maintain his carriage.

This is the very moment of ending the trot and beginning the walk.

UPWARD TRANSITIONS

- Allow the horse to go forwards by softening your body. Don't give away the rein contact, as this throws him off balance and out of shape, which makes it harder for him.
- Teach the horse to do good upward transitions by doing as little as possible yourself: a good way to tune the horse up to this is to repeat the same transition a few times, one after the other, giving lighter aids with each repetition.
- 'Ask' and let the horse take you up, rather than you taking responsibility by pushing him into a higher gait.
- Pick a good moment to ask for an upward transition: that is, when he is listening and balanced.
- Wait until the gait you are in is good before asking for an upward transition, as a bad walk leads to a bad trot or canter. A good walk gives you a better chance of going up into a good trot or canter.

- Avoid squeezing with the legs, as this clamps the horse's body. This is like driving a car with one foot on the accelerator and one foot on the brake at the same time… instead, tune him up by using a very light leg, then a couple of tiny touches of the stick: 'tap-tap'.
- Think of it being the horse's hind legs that start the upward transition.
- An upward transition does not necessarily mean the horse has to go faster, it is simply asking him to change the sequence in which he is using his legs: walk has a four-time beat, trot has a two-time and canter a three-time beat; however, theoretically all three paces can be ridden at the same speed.

Fantastique is walking well behind. I am shortening her a little too much in front as she is anticipating my thought to trot again.

The first stride of the new trot, although her outside hind is a little late coming through.

The new trot: notice how the trot has more elevation and spring than the trot in picture 1, as a result of the preceding downward and upward transitions.

WALK TRANSITIONS

- Ride an exact number of steps in walk – for example, six – and then halt.
- Repeat this sequence, feeling for more connection between you and the horse… see if you can give lighter and lighter aids with each repeat of the walk and halt to teach him to be more responsive to you.
- Notice if he puts his head more to one side than the other, and use the reins to straighten him.
- Notice if he puts his quarters to one side or the other, in which case bring his shoulders across with both reins, so they are in front of his quarters.

TROT TRANSITIONS

- To refine upward transitions to trot, try releasing the inside of your upper thighs, and give a couple of light touches with the stick if you need to, but don't squeeze with your legs. As we have seen, squeezing with the lower leg tightens your back and thighs, almost asking the horse *not* to go at the same time as asking him to go.
- Try doing transitions from collected trot to forward working trot and back again. This increases the horse's power and elasticity in the trot. It also gets him really listening to your seat and body.
- It is especially useful to practise trot to halt to trot, or even trot to reinback to trot. This ultimately leads to piaffe, the most collected form of trot, but meanwhile it really improves the horse's responses and carriage, and opens up his extended trot.

Fantastique has a fairly forward walk, and she can 'hear me' thinking about cantering.

She strikes off immediately from the walk into canter, with her hindquarters nicely engaged, although she has braced her neck a little too much.

CANTER TRANSITIONS

- Wait for a good moment to ask for canter.
- If the horse gets tense doing canter transitions, do something else for a while, and then come back to it.
- Don't rush the horse into canter… think about the one-two-three leg sequence and teach him to go into canter without running in trot. If he runs in trot before cantering, bring him back to a slow trot and ask for canter again.
- Go into canter in the same place a few times, until the horse has got the idea.
- Coming down from canter, it is worth teaching the horse to come to a walk or stop, rather than falling into a fast trot on his forehand.
- Horses learn by repetition, so to improve the canter transitions, ride a big circle (20m) and repeat lots of transitions in and out of canter: for example, canter only eight strides, then walk eight, then canter eight, and so on.
- Ultimately you want the horse to go into canter *instantly* from a tiny inside leg aid on the correct canter lead (right lead or left lead) on a straight line or a circle… and when he can do that calmly and smoothly, he will be ready to begin learning the flying change!

Her frame is shortened, and she is higher in front as she prepares herself to canter.

You can see what happens if the horse is not ready for a transition: here I have surprised Fantastique with the aid to canter, so she is finding it difficult to balance and be round in her carriage.

The Perfect Rider Checklist

- Be precise about where you ask for a transition, and also about what speed and type of pace you want: for example, don't just ask for 'trot', ask for a specific trot speed and type of trot before you ask for the transition.
- Pay attention to staying in balance through transitions: if you tip forwards you interfere with the horse's forehand, and if you tip back, you make him have to wait for you to 'catch him up', or you influence his back so that it dips down rather than rounds up.
- Don't surprise the horse with a transition request.

USING YOUR VOICE

Horses are sensitive to sound, and it can be useful to use sound as a temporary tool for transitions: saying 'walk on', 'trot on' or 'can-ter' in an uplifting tone, or clicking your tongue, can help the horse know you want an upward transition.

Making a low, dropping tone, or saying 'e-a-s-y' or 'whoa', or whistling in a tone that drops down in pitch, can help downward transitions; and sighing can also be very effective for downward transitions.

Perry's Tips

- Horses are creatures of habit with a great memory, which means you can use the horse's natural inclination to anticipate a transition in a certain place as a way to get his transitions going better; so for example, if you always ask for canter at the same corner of the arena, he will begin to offer it to you at that corner out of habit.
- If the horse starts making too many assumptions by anticipating a change of gait in a particular place, change your plan of action and ride past the spot where he was anticipating, without doing a transition.

FLYING CHANGES

A

The reason why flying changes are in this chapter about smooth transitions is that a flying change is actually nothing more than a canter transition: it is just that the horse is already cantering on the other lead when you ask him.

The flying change is when the horse changes his canter lead from one to the other, right or left, whilst maintaining the canter. The change happens in the moment of suspension in the canter, when all four of his legs are in the air. The flying change is a natural movement for the horse, one that he most often uses when changing direction whilst cantering or galloping at liberty – you can even see young foals performing this movement.

It is important to remember that flying changes can be mentally, physically and emotionally demanding upon the horse (and sometimes the rider), so they should not be asked for too much.

B

A) This is the moment before the flying change. We have just come around the corner on the right canter lead at letter M, and now head across the arena towards letter K. I have given a half-halt to collect Fantastique. My leg is in position to move her quarters a tiny bit away from the camera: she is well established in her changes, so I do not need to actually move her quarters over, but she and I are both thinking it, which prepares her to change.

B) This shows the actual flying change: the moment in the air when the horse switches all four of her legs ready for the new canter lead. I have brought my leg forwards to the girth, releasing the horse's quarters and allowing her to change. I have also turned my hips slightly to indicate the new canter lead. I have not done anything active with my hands, as I don't want to get in her way or throw her front across with the reins.

PREPARATION

The secret to successful flying changes is in the preparation. Assuming your horse is physically sound and strong enough, there are three main things to prepare in order to achieve the flying change:

1. The horse should do *instant* walk-to-canter transitions, 100 per cent reliably on either canter lead. Once the horse responds instantly to your request to canter on either canter lead from a walk or halt, he should respond the same when you are already cantering.
2. You want a nice 'bouncy' forward canter, with plenty of time spent in the air in each bound of the canter.
3. The horse should also yield his hindquarters away from your leg nicely in canter, so teaching the half-pass in canter is a good preparation (see 'Dances the Lateral Movements', page 122).

☐ HOW TO DO IT - IN THE RIDING ARENA

You cannot make a horse do a flying change, but you can set things up for him so he offers it to you. There are various ways to first introduce a horse to flying changes. Perhaps the most common way that people try is to ride a figure-of-eight in the arena with a 'simple change' (a few strides of trot or walk, then taking the other canter lead) in the centre as they change direction. Here is a slight variation, which has the advantage of the horse pushing off from his hind legs as he comes out of the corner of the arena:

1. Canter round the 'short side' of the arena in true canter, and as you come out of the second corner ride as though you are going to go across the school along the long diagonal – for example, letter M to letter K – then ask the horse to walk for a couple of strides.
2. In the two walk strides, change his bend by changing your hips and leg position. Bring what was your outside leg forwards to the girth and put your inside leg behind the girth.
3. Now ask the horse to go into canter again on the other canter lead.
4. Repeat steps 1–3 in the same place in the arena until the horse starts anticipating the transition up from the walk to the new canter lead.
5. Now it is time to ask for the flying change. Instead of coming back to the walk as you have been doing half-halt to shorten the horse's stride and let him know something is coming, then use your outside leg behind the girth to push the horse's hindquarters sideways a little (like a mini half-pass) for a couple of strides. At the spot where you have been changing his bend and asking for the new canter lead, release your outside leg forwards to the girth and allow the horse to pick up the new canter lead.

If you get a clean change, let the horse rest and stop work for the day. If you don't get a clean change, it probably means more preparation is required to make him more responsive to the transition aids.

6. Once the horse is familiar with the aids and timing of the flying change in one place, I will begin asking for it in different parts of the arena. When the flying change is well established between you, it is reasonably straightforward to ask for multiple changes – every four, three or two strides – and this is an excellent way to improve your timing, too.
7. Over the following weeks and months we will be repeating and refining the movement, but always making sure things stay pretty calm, as flying changes can make horses get over-anxious, tense or excited.

C) Beginnings the new canter lead, now cantering on the left lead towards letter K.

The horse is on the right lead and feeling pretty keen. She is wanting to head off past the left of the camera, but my leg is holding her from going that way by asking her hindquarters to move slightly away from the camera. Note we are cantering along the side of a gentle slope too, which is not so easy for her on this lead.

The moment of the flying change. I have released my leg forwards, turned my hips, and agreed with her that we can head off up the hill past the camera, which allows her to change canter leads. Notice I am riding one-handed with a curb bit. Riding flying changes one-handed is a good way to make sure you don't try pulling the horse around to change.

The first stride of the new (left) canter lead. You can see how much power was contained within Fantastique's wish to change lead and head off up the slope!

☐ HOW TO DO IT – OUTDOORS

In this method I begin by using the horse's natural desire to magnetize towards something, for example home, or one of his friends. (It is only advisable to use this method when you can easily control the pace of the canter, regardless of whether the horse is heading towards or away from his desired destination!)

1. I canter towards somewhere the horse wants to go.
2. With my 'outside' leg behind the girth, I ask him to yield sideways two or three steps (canter half-pass, see 'Dances the Lateral Movements, page 129), so my leg is now gently holding him a couple of degrees away from where he wants to go.
3. I then bring that leg forward towards the girth as I allow him to head for his desired destination again. This is the moment he is likely to offer a flying change, at which point if he does, I will ask him to walk, and will then relax the reins and take him home.

TIPS TO HELP WITH FLYING CHANGES

- Only start asking for the flying change when the horse is excellent at all of the things listed above in 'Preparation'. And if the flying changes are not working, go back to improving these things before trying again.
- Keep your hands still. It can be tempting to try and throw the horse across to the other canter lead with the hands, but they are more likely to get in the way and make him change his front legs before his hind legs, and this can be a difficult habit to get rid of.
- Avoid big movements or throwing your weight about: these can make it difficult for the horse to change.

- Don't surprise him, or give strong aids.
- Look to your timing: say to yourself 'three, two, one, *change*' with each bound of canter, and then your new canter aids (leg and seat position) should be in place on the word 'change', not after it.
- Don't look down to check if the change has happened: train yourself to feel which canter lead you are on without looking. Do this at first by feeling the horse's forelegs reaching forwards whilst in walk. When you can really feel this, practise feeling for the forelegs in canter: the sensation is very similar.

Remember that doing transitions, and particularly flying changes, are hard work for the horse, so it is also important to include transitions down from hard work to chill-out time as part of your routine!

✓ DOs

- Be very clear about what, where and when you want your transitions.
- Ask very quietly, and wait.
- Know exactly what gait and tempo you want after the transition.

✗ DON'Ts

- Don't raise your heels, kick or squeeze to 'go'.
- Don't brace your back too much to slow down or stop, because it will cause the horse to dip his back.

Wonderful Paces

Have you ever stood and watched a herd of horses leaping, dancing and playing at liberty in the pasture on a windy day? I think most people would agree it is an awesome sight – even an 'old plodder' can come alive and turn into a wild stallion, throwing himself into airs above the ground with the sheer joy of movement. In these moments, you can look on with awe at extended trots that float, and pirouettes, spins and lightning-speed transitions performed with amazing power, balance and grace.

There is no doubt that some horses are born with more impressive and fantastic paces than others, but I think most people would agree that every horse can look amazing when leaping, dancing and playing in the pasture with his friends. This theoretically means they can do it with a rider on board, too, and that is what we aim for (within reason) when we train the horse.

At least as important as how the horse's paces look when he moves, is how they feel to the rider. What I want to feel from my horse's paces is rhythmic, balanced, powerful and fluid movement. That is what we are aiming towards with much of the work the horse and I do together.

In this chapter we will explore some of the many ways you can improve the paces of your horse.

TO IMPROVE THE WALK

- To achieve a nice swinging walk, rather than squeezing and pushing with your seat and legs, teach the horse to stride out on a long rein by releasing your hips and thighs, then use light touches of the stick. Time the stick to touch his hindquarters (usually the 'inside' hind leg) just as the corresponding hind hoof is leaving the ground; that way he is able to respond by stepping deeper under his body with the leg, giving you a much more forward walk.

- To create more impulsion in the walk, do a circuit or two of canter, then come back to the walk, but maintain the raised energy level from the faster pace.

- For more energy and purpose in the walk, trot a 20m circle, then walk four or five strides before trotting again, all the while thinking about the next trot. Come to walk again in the same place. Repeat this a few times and see the energy build in the walk (see Calm, Willing and Forward-going, page 48). Once the energy has built, do your best to flow with the extra movement of the horse's back, to teach him to stay in that type of forward walk.

- Lateral work such as the shoulder-in, done very slowly in walk, can improve the forwardness and expression in the walk once you ride straight again.

- If the walk is too hurried or strung out, walk a few small circles (about 8m).

- To collect the walk, rather than stiffening your body (which can decrease the horse's impulsion), relax your lower back a little, whilst *thinking* tall, have your heels lowered, release your hips, keep the rein contact light but asking, and wait for the horse to collect himself within the framework you have created with your body, legs and the reins. Remember that collection requires forward energy, which is gathered up.

Fantastique is striding out well here, stepping quite deeply under her body with her hind legs and reaching forwards into the bridle by extending her neck. This picture shows the exact moment to touch with the stick on the inside: just as her inside hind hoof is leaving the ground. You don't have to actually look at the hind legs to know when to touch with the stick: as the horse's hind leg leaves the ground you will feel his side (ribs) going inwards.

Once you have enough energy in the walk it becomes possible to gather that energy and create a more collected walk. It is important when collecting the walk that you pick up the rein contact without blocking the flow of energy by bracing with your body or legs.

Rising to the trot (posting) can help the horse to trot freely forwards.

TO IMPROVE THE TROT

The trot is the pace used most for improving the horse's way of going. Unlike the walk, the trot has more natural impulsion; and unlike the canter, which is a one-sided gait because of the sequence of the horse's footfalls, the trot is a 'straight' gait, in that the legs move together in evenly matched pairs. The other advantage the trot has over canter is that the trot is not a gait the horse naturally uses to run away from danger, so in trot he can be less reactive.

- Because the trot is usually the easiest gait in which to achieve an even rhythm from the horse, it can be useful to ask him to trot continuously for a while (say, five minutes or more, depending on fitness) until he settles into a nice forward-going pace.

- At the opposite end of the scale from trotting for longer periods, also have times when you ask for only six, eight or ten strides of trot before returning to walk, as a way of making sure he balances himself in front and does not just 'go to sleep' while he trots.

- Do rising trot to help the horse into a free forward trot. When rising to the trot, try letting your heels bounce down every time you rise and every time you sit. Make sure when you sit it is softly and your seat comes down in the front of the saddle near the pommel, not hitting the back near the cantle.

- When doing rising trot, try having your hands quite wide apart and think of your body coming forwards towards the horse's ears, rather than upwards.

- In both rising and sitting trot, to help the horse move more freely, try relaxing the contact your knees have with the saddle flaps. Think of your knees as 'floating' rather than gripping.

- To improve the roundness of the horse's trot, try riding lots of trot-walk-trot transitions, making sure the horse responds to lighter and lighter aids and stays in the same outline. Once the horse is really responsive, you can take it further by asking him for trot-halt-trot transitions in the same way. Finally, try riding trot-reinback-trot transitions; this will really help him to engage his hind legs underneath him and is an exercise which can eventually lead to the piaffe (see picture below).

Really open up the trot by asking for some piaffe-like steps, and then let the horse go fully forwards in a big trot.

Look at how the horse moves at liberty to see what kind of trot he has and how he moves naturally in that gait – without a rider. Fantastique has a very expressive trot, which tells me I may potentially be able to experience some fantastic trot work with her.

- It is fairly pointless just trotting round and round for the sake of it: the horse gets bored and so does the rider! When doing your trot work, really feel the horse… feel his rhythm, feel his balance, feel how he is stepping up from behind, feel if he is leaning on the reins, feel if he is going straight or crooked… By feeling these things as the horse trots, you and he will begin having a 'listening' dialogue which makes things interesting, because no two trot strides are ever exactly the same.
- There is an endless variety of different trots, and each horse can give you many variations. Instead of always letting the horse choose the trot he prefers (which is probably because it is the one in which he can do the least work), make it a habit to ask for different paces of trot from him. If he is very forward in trot, it can improve him by asking sometimes for a very shortened trot; and if he is quite low in energy in trot, it can help to ask for real forwardness in trot on straight lines, perhaps going uphill outdoors somewhere, with his friends ahead of him disappearing out of sight!

- To increase the power and impulsion of the trot, ride a few trot-canter-trot transitions.
- To make the trot more alive, frequently vary the pattern you ride – go from small circle to big circle or straight lines, then back again.
- Avoid sitting to the trot unless the horse is round in his back, otherwise it can be uncomfortable for horse and rider. Ask the horse to collect or round himself a little in the walk, before easing him up into trot, so that he is already round in his back before you start, and stays that way as you go into trot.
- See if you can ask for the trot with your legs and then let the legs be quiet as much as possible. Constantly nagging legs in trot is a very common habit but it can get in the way of the horse's ability to really swing in the trot.
- Make sure the horse trots at your tempo and not his own, but be sure your tempo is reasonable for the horse's stage of development…Some horses go slow in the trot to save themselves working, and some horses rush in the trot to save themselves from engaging behind.

For medium and extended trots it can be a mistake to push the horse on with legs, stick or spurs during the movement, as this gets in his way. What is needed is to build the power and energy before extending, and then all you are doing is releasing him to really burst forwards in trot. This is what we have done here, by building the energy in the previous corner, and then allowing it to power forwards.

TO IMPROVE THE CANTER

Have a look at how your horse moves in canter without the rider; this can give you a lot of insight into what you might expect to achieve when riding the horse. It is interesting to notice which canter lead the horse prefers when at liberty, as this will be the same under saddle.

- To ask for canter, place the outside leg back quietly, the inside leg on the girth, half-halt to collect the horse for a moment, then ask him to canter with your inside leg.
- Probably the most common problem with getting into canter is that the rider thinks canter means 'go faster', and that is what they unconsciously ask the horse to do. Once the horse is rushing (going fast on his forehand) in trot, it is not always very easy for him to actually find his balance and to canter.
- Provided the horse is fit enough and at a suitable stage of his education, I may canter for a long time without a break – for example, for five or more minutes – to allow him to find his balance and rhythm.
- I also work on cantering only a few strides at a time to get the canter more elastic: for example, ride a 20m circle and canter for exactly ten, eight or six strides, then walk for six, then canter for the same number again, then walk for six, and so on – basically, plenty of repeated canter transitions.

NOTE: Please remember that these are demanding exercises for the horse, and – like every exercise in this book – should only be practised in accordance with the horse's level of development, fitness and ability.

Fantastique is giving me a nice elastic canter here and is quite collected. Although she is a little behind the vertical with her head, she is not evading the bridle.

- Improve the canter by going up into canter from walk rather than from trot.
- In canter, try gradually spiralling in from a 20m circle to as small a circle as you can without losing the canter, then leg-yield the horse back out on to the big circle.
- Try riding the occasional smaller circle in canter (maybe 8 or10m), as this helps to bring the canter more 'together' and collected.
- When lateral work is well established, riding travers and then half-pass in canter will take this gait to a new level (see 'Dances the Lateral Movements', page 129).
- To get more 'go' in the canter, try riding counter canter, then true canter again. (Counter canter is when the horse's leading leg is to the outside of the circle or arena for example, going round to the right whilst cantering on the *left* lead, or going left on the *right* lead).
- If you have trouble getting a particular canter lead, it often means the horse is weak or uncomfortable in his 'outside' hindquarter; so rather than hammering away at trying to get the difficult canter lead, perhaps have a vet or chiropractor check him out, and then do more work to supple and strengthen him on the other rein. For example, if he has trouble getting right lead in canter, work on circles, small circles, transitions and shoulder-in on the left rein, in order to strengthen his left hindquarter.

The counter canter can really help loosen up the horse's true canter. Here Fantastique is being ridden on the left rein (anti-clockwise around the arena) but is actually on the right canter lead.

IMPROVING THE PACES WHEN RIDING OUT

1

In walk: Explore and enjoy the horse's free, forward-going walk while out riding, allowing him to swing his back nicely, especially on the way home (picture 1). Theoretically, if the horse can swing in the walk in that kind of situation, he can do it anywhere.

In trot: Use the horse's desire to go forwards when riding outdoors to collect his trot (picture 2). As we have seen, collection is about gathering in the energy, which can be a lot easier outdoors where there is more impulsion readily available to tap into.

Use the horse's forwardness and extra energy outside to open him up and increase the power and extension in the trot, especially on uphill slopes.

In canter: You can use the horse's desire to 'go' out riding to collect him and actually get slower canters outside than in the school (picture 3).

Perfect Rider Checklist

- In the walk, make sure your legs are nice and loose on the horse to help him walk freely.
- In the trot, make sure you don't have the very common habit of kicking or squeezing with the legs at every stride: the perfect riding horse should not need this – you ask him to trot and he trots, without you having to work all the time: constant use of the legs can take away some of the brilliance in the trot, and can limit his forwardness, too.
- Have long heels (heels gently lowered).
- Have your knees turned gently in towards the saddle, but without gripping.
- In the canter, be soft in the waist, so your seat goes with the horse's movement: avoid pushing with the seat as this makes the canter somewhat 'wooden'. Impulsion in the canter comes from a leg aid or a touch of the stick, not the rider pushing into the horse's back.
- Remind yourself that canter doesn't necessarily mean going fast!

✓ DOs
- It is important to spend time working on your horse's paces.
- Remember it can take time to bring out the brilliance in some horses' paces.
- Take a really close look at how your horse moves when he is at liberty or on the lunge: see what he does well, and where he looks a bit 'sticky'.

✗ DON'Ts
- Don't be in a hurry or try to force the brilliance out of the horse: it will look and feel much better when he gives it to you himself as a result of months and even years of training.
- Don't forget that each horse is naturally better at one pace than another: thus some are fantastic in trot and harder in canter, some are the other way round.

Dances the Lateral Movements

The term 'lateral movement'
refers to the various ways
we can ask the horse to
go sideways and forwards
at the same time. Lateral
movements can transform
a riding horse: they increase
suppleness, softness, roundness,
responsiveness and strength –
they even improve forwardness.
In fact, some ridden problems
may simply disappear if you
practise lateral movements
regularly.

For many people the term 'lateral movement' may conjure
up images of top class dressage horses and dancing Spanish
stallions, but there are many situations where any riding
horse will be required to move sideways, for example at
gates, to avoid objects or bad footing, or to be under better
control in traffic.

Many riders avoid lateral work because it is perceived to
be advanced or too difficult, but if taken in simple steps as
described in this chapter it is quite attainable by anybody, and
adds a new dimension to the horse's skills. The four lateral
movements with the most value to us in creating the perfect
riding horse are shoulder-in, travers, renvers and half-pass.

THE SHOULDER-IN

In the shoulder-in, the horse moves with his hind legs on the track and his forehand (shoulders) brought in a little off the track, meaning he goes sideways and forwards at the same time. He should be bent round the rider's inside leg (the leg he moves away from) with his head bent slightly *away* from the direction he is going in.

Shoulder-in can be performed in walk or trot. I suggest you begin teaching the horse in a slow walk, so he has time to think about what you are asking, and you can 'feel' more of what he is doing underneath you. (When the horse is first learning lateral work I don't worry too much about losing impulsion: it will increase again afterwards.)

THREE- OR FOUR-TRACK SHOULDER-IN?

There is a lot of discussion about the merits of riding three- or four-track shoulder-in, but to my mind they both have benefits for the horse, which means we can use one or the other, depending on what benefit we want.

The three-track shoulder-in (required in dressage competitions) is ridden at a shallower angle than the four-track, with the horse moving more forwards than sideways, so if you were to stand on the track in front of him you would see only three of his legs (the inside hind leg is hidden because it is following the line of the outside foreleg). Instead of the hind legs crossing each other, they move straight and come well forwards underneath the horse's belly; this improves the horse's strength in his hindquarters while maintaining forward impulsion.

In four-track shoulder-in, the horse is ridden with more angle from the side of the arena, so if you were to stand on the track in front of him you would see all four of his legs, making four tracks on the arena surface (see picture above). In four-track shoulder-in the horse's hind legs cross each other more; this helps his hips to become more flexible, and it also helps him to come more deeply on the bit.

EXERCISE 1
COUNTER SHOULDER-IN IN HAND

Teaching your horse this kind of exercise in hand can help him (and you) to understand the movement before riding it. To help the horse understand shoulder-in, we are first going to show him counter shoulder-in. This is the same movement as shoulder-in, except that the horse's forehand faces the wall or fence of the arena, which makes things more obvious for the horse, and gives *you* less to think about it, too… and once he has learned counter shoulder-in, it will be easier to ask him for shoulder-in.

HOW TO DO IT

1. Stand on the outside of your horse (between him and the fence), hold the outside rein about four inches from the bit (we will call this your 'rein hand') and have the other hand (we will call this the 'stick hand') near the girth, holding the other rein (which comes up over his wither). The stick is held near the horse's hindquarters. Calmly and *slowly* walk on the track with the horse to the inside of the arena, which means you are walking between the horse and the fence.
2. Ask the horse to yield his head towards you with the 'rein hand', and ask him to yield his body away from you with your 'stick hand', using a light touch at the girth where your leg will be when you ride him. Support this with little touches of the stick on his hindquarters if necessary.
3. Keep walking rhythmically and facing down the track, with the horse at a shallow angle to the fence, making three or four tracks with his legs and feet when he is viewed from the front (see the picture below).

Perfect Rider Checklist

- Every time you ask for something, begin by asking with very light aids; if you need to, repeat your request, and then gradually increase the intensity of your 'ask' until the horse responds.
- With every exercise, always remember to practise the same on both sides of the horse.
- As a rule for the lateral movements, turn yourself (including your head) so you are aligned with the horse's body and looking in the same direction he is.
- You need a very clear idea or picture in your mind about precisely what the lateral movement you are asking for looks like before you start.

EXERCISE 2
COUNTER SHOULDER-IN UNDER SADDLE

HOW TO DO IT

1. As you approach the long side of the arena where you intend to counter shoulder-in, picture the movement in your mind, so the horse can prepare himself.
2. Let your seat and legs flow with the roll of his belly and barrel, and as you come to the long side, subtly change his bend a little to the outside, so he now bends round your *outside* leg at the girth and his head is slightly flexed to the outside.
3. Your inside leg is held passively, a little behind the girth to support his quarters.
4. Have your body facing outside the arena at the same angle you want the horse to perform the movement, which means you look between his ears.
5. Stay over his centre of balance as he moves forwards and sideways simultaneously along the fence.

EXERCISE 3
SHOULDER-IN IN HAND

Once the horse has grasped the idea of counter shoulder-in, he should find it quite easy to understand the three- and four-track shoulder-in.

Once again we will start by asking for the movement in hand. This time we walk on the inside of the horse (he is on the track between you and the fence) and ask his forehand (shoulders) to come in towards the school a little.

Perry's Tips

- Most things we do with horses work best if we prepare them, and then allow them to get on with it. With lateral work, prepare the horse by creating the angle and bend you want, and then let him carry out the movement. It is much easier to prepare the horse well, rather than try and fix something while he performs it!
- Practise keeping your hands light so the reins don't become braced or stiff between you and the horse.

HOW TO DO IT

1. Hold the inside rein about four inches from the bit, and have the other hand near the girth, holding the outside rein (which comes over his wither), along with the stick (which rests near the side of the horse's hindquarters).
2. Calmly and slowly walk down the side of the arena, with the horse walking straight beside you on the track.
3. After the corner, use *both hands* to bring his forehand into the arena a little, so he is walking with his 'shoulders in' and his hindquarters still on the track.
4. If he stops, use your 'stick hand' lightly at the girth, or a very delicate touch of the stick on his quarters to ask him to keep walking with you.

EXERCISE 4
SHOULDER-IN UNDER SADDLE

HOW TO DO IT

1. About 10 metres before you are going to ask for shoulder-in, picture the horse doing the movement in your mind to let him know something is going to happen.
2. Your inside leg should passively follow the 'in-out' movement of his belly as he moves; this will be your leg aid during the shoulder-in.
3. As the horse turns the corner, turn as though both of you were about to ride straight across the school on the long diagonal.
4. Whilst keeping a slight bend of his head to the inside, have a momentary 'feel' (half-halt) on the outside rein, just as the outside foreleg goes forwards. This tells the horse you don't want to go across the school, and will make him redirect his energy into moving sideways into the shoulder-in.
5. Stay over the horse's centre of gravity, and go with him as he performs the movement.

SHOULDER-IN ON THE CIRCLE

I sometimes ride the shoulder-in on a big circle (usually 20 metres): this increases the flexing of the horse's hips, and puts him more deeply on the bit, as you can see here. The drawbacks of this movement are the possible loss of impulsion, or the horse going on to his forehand; however, you can really see from these pictures how good this movement is for the gymnastic ability of the horse.

Perry's Tips

- If the shoulder-in goes wrong, ride a small circle, prepare the horse and start the movement again.
- In the shoulder-in, as much as possible avoid using the inside rein because this spoils the movement. If you want to increase the angle, or ask for more engagement of the hindquarters in the shoulder-in, have another feel on the *outside* rein, ideally just as his outside shoulder goes forwards.
- Timing is everything: almost!

THE HALF-PASS, TRAVERS AND RENVERS

The half-pass is the pinnacle of lateral movements, requiring the rider and horse to work in true partnership. It is a fabulous way to increase your horse's strength, collection and athleticism. It can be performed in walk, trot or canter. In the half-pass, the horse dances across the arena, moving sideways and forwards, looking in the direction he is going, whilst engaging and swinging his legs and back. Unlike shoulder-in or leg-yield, where it is easier for the rider to push the horse into performing the movement, in the half-pass the rider *invites* the horse to perform.

The half-pass is a more demanding and athletic movement than we have looked at so far, so the horse should be well warmed up and supple before beginning. If your horse has already learned the shoulder-in very well, you will have a good chance of achieving a successful half-pass.

NOTE: Any lateral movements, but especially half-pass, should only be practised in line with the horse's level of fitness and training by gradually building him up.

The half-pass in trot. My outside leg (left leg) is behind the girth, and my inside leg (right leg) is quite far forwards, 'allowing' the horse to move forwards and sideways to the right.

EXERCISE 5
TRAVERS

In the same way that the arena fence in counter shoulder-in helped the horse to understand shoulder-in, we will use the fence by doing travers first. This will help the horse to understand the movement and the aids of half-pass. In travers the horse travels along the side of the arena with his forehand on the track, his head facing the direction of travel, and his hindquarters a little towards the inside of the school. He is bent round the rider's leg, into which he is moving. This is basically the same movement as half-pass, but performed on the outside track of the arena.

HOW TO DO IT

1. As you travel along the short side of the arena, picture the horse in travers along the next long side, to let him know what you are intending. Lighten your inside leg a little and have the outside leg behind the girth, following the 'in-out' swing of the horse's ribs.
2. Think of the travers starting as you approach the corner *before* the long side of the arena, so your body faces towards the fence on the long side and you keep the horse's head bent to the inside using light reins. This means both of you are angled slightly towards the fence with your bodies, and both of you are looking down the long side towards the next corner.
3. Having previously taught the horse to flex his head round to our leg (see 'Soft Mouth', page 78), place your inside leg well forwards on the girth so he bends round it, but light enough that he still moves *into* it.
4. Keep the outside leg behind the girth, passively asking the horse to move sideways with his quarters.

EXERCISE 6
THE HALF-PASS UNDER SADDLE

HOW TO DO IT

1. With the horse tracking right, establish a good bend in the horse to the right, then leave the track at letter **C** and turn on to the centre line of the arena.
2. Have your outside leg (left leg) behind the girth, your inside leg (right leg) quite forwards on the girth, and turn the horse's head to the right – along with your head – to face letter **E**.
3. Give an initial leg aid with the outside leg to ask the horse to go sideways, then – while you and the horse continue to look at letter **E** – ride towards it, maintaining the sideways angle established at the beginning of the movement, with the horse's shoulders slightly ahead of the hindquarters.
4. Repeat on the left.

EXERCISE 7
RENVERS

In renvers the horse moves in the same way as he does in the half-pass and travers, but now he travels on the track of the arena with his hindquarters towards the fence or wall and his head to the inside of the school. He is still looking in the direction of travel, and is bent around the leg on that side.

I usually leave renvers until the last of all the lateral movements, as sometimes the horse seems to find it harder to understand than shoulder-in, half-pass or travers. Renvers has a very useful collecting effect on the horse. Unlike travers, where the horse's head is following the fence and he may be more likely to 'lean' on it a little and therefore be lower in front, in renvers his forehand is away from the fence so he isn't able to use it for support.

Like half-pass and travers, renvers can be performed in walk, trot and canter.

HOW TO DO IT

By the time we come to ask for renvers, the horse will be quite supple and manoeuvrable, so he shouldn't find this movement too difficult.

1. Ride a counter shoulder-in at the beginning of the long side of the arena, which means you will be facing the fence.
2. After a few strides, maintain the same bend in the horse but turn yourself (and the horse should come with you) to face the inside of the arena.
3. Now the horse will be in renvers.

TIPS FOR RIDING LATERAL MOVEMENTS OUTDOORS

- Use natural features to flex or supple the horse.
- Ride lateral movements on lanes and tracks, where appropriate, to keep your horse listening.

✓ DOs
- Do enjoy the moments when the horse starts to perform and feels fantastic as a result of the training you are doing with him.

✗ DON'Ts
- Don't get strong, frustrated, or be in a hurry: creating a light, responsive and obedient horse takes time (months and years), and is on-going work done every time you ride.

Beautiful Self-carriage and Collection

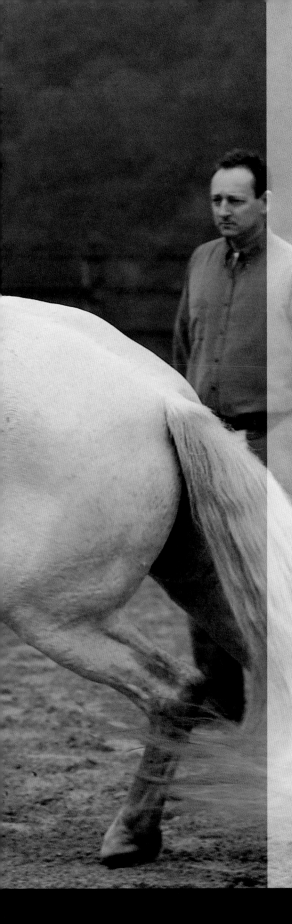

We all know how wonderfully horses can move when they dance, leap and have fun at liberty together. If you want to see how incredible the horse's carriage can be, watch him on a wild windy day as he plays and prances with his buddies: he will arch his neck, lift his back, pump up his topline, and push forwards and up off his powerful hindquarters. What we are ultimately aiming for is to re-create some of that awesome self-carriage when we sit on him.

The horse is in 'self-carriage' when he is collected (on the bit) without you having to actively work to keep him there with your hands or legs: he is bringing his hocks well forwards underneath his body, and his back and neck are arched so he looks really beautiful.

Good self-carriage and collection have many benefits for both horse and rider, regardless of the type of riding being enjoyed. Good carriage is better for the horse's back, because it is a stronger way of carrying the rider's weight; the horse becomes more athletic and capable; he is more comfortable for the rider; and the aids and communication between the horse and rider become much more refined.

Since mind and body are intrinsically linked — particularly in horses — self-carriage is not just about the horse's body, it is also about his state of mind. A horse in self-carriage is attuned to each tiny request from the rider, and is a sheer joy to ride.

THE TERMS 'COLLECTION' AND 'ON THE BIT'

'Collection' is when the horse's forward energy from his hindquarters is gathered and used to lift his back and forehand upwards, making him more athletic and with more spring in his paces and movement.

Rather than work hard myself to get the horse to collect, I much prefer to set things up so the horse finds the answer for himself and seeks to be on the bit by choice. Here is an example of self-carriage where I have set things up and am basically doing nothing other than riding the motion of Fantastique's wonderful forward trot, staying soft in my body and legs and keeping 'out of her way' as much as possible. The rein contact is light, and impulsion is coming through beautifully from her hindquarters.

See how Fantastique has her haunches quite forwards underneath her body, and as a result her forehand is raised. When the horse moves like this, his body is shortened and compressed, and it feels like sitting on a coiled spring, with much of the weight of both horse and rider carried on the horse's hindquarters.

The term 'on the bit' is very often misunderstood, as it implies that it is simply about the horse's head position. What it actually means is that the horse is actively bringing his hocks well forwards underneath his body, lengthening his 'topline' or back, and carrying more of his weight on his hindquarters. All this has the effect of lightening his forehand, of getting him to flex more at the poll (the point between his ears), and of creating an arched neck and near-vertical head position. When the horse works in this way the rein contact becomes light and even in the rider's hands, his back feels more elastic and arched, and his movement feels smoother to ride.

Perry's Tips

- Although it is good for developing the horse's body, I do not agree with riding the horse on the bit all the time, particularly when riding outdoors. Even in the arena it is good practice to give the horse things to do and rest periods, so he has a chance to stretch out and relax his body.

- It isn't necessary to push hard with the legs or have a strong contact in order to get a horse collected or on the bit. Subtle riding and long-term training of the horse are what make him light, supple and strong in his body.

CREATING SELF-CARRIAGE

Most of the qualities for the perfect riding horse that we have looked at so far in this book have been bringing us nearer to having a horse in self-carriage. You need lightness in the mouth and responsiveness to the leg and seat, also suppleness in the horse's body, impulsion, and some energy there for you to collect.

Circles, turns, lateral movements, transitions and riding into the corners of the arena all help to collect and 'round' the horse. In the picture, left, Fantastique's inside hind has to step well under her body in the corner during the second beat of the canter, and as a result she is raising her forehand nicely. The corner is also helping me to contain some of her excess forward energy and turn it into collection.

In this trot (below) I am placing Fantastique's forehand very slightly to the inside of the arena, which is creating a soft bend and encouraging her to be on the bit in self-carriage. The soft bend is requiring her to engage her inside hind leg a little more, rather like riding a turn or circle. I am bringing the forehand in a little by having the inside leg lightly at the girth and both reins being held a tiny bit towards the inside of the school – although the outside rein does not cross over the wither.

THE HALF-HALT

The half-halt is a momentary pause within the forward motion of the horse, which has the effect of collecting and rebalancing him.

☐ HOW TO DO IT

- Deepen your legs.
- Put a little more 'tone' in your spine for a brief moment (without going stiff).
- Perhaps have a 'feel' on one rein (usually the outside rein). Give the rein aid as the outside foreleg steps forwards.

These three aids effectively ask the horse's forehand to slow and the hindquarters to keep coming through, creating better balance and lift in the horse's carriage. You can see in the picture at left how I have deepened my legs, so the horse is using her hind legs well; I have made my spine a little firmer for this one stride and given a 'feel' on the outside rein; all of which has the effect of bringing the horse up together more in the canter. In the next stride I will relax my back and allow her to continue forwards.

STRETCHING FORWARDS

It is sometimes useful to ask the horse to really stretch forwards towards the bridle with his whole frame, as a way of opening his back and getting him to step freely and deeply underneath himself with his hind legs. Once the horse is stepping deeply under his body with his hind legs, reaching well into the bridle and stretching his spine, quietly shorten the reins without changing anything else, to transform the stretch into more collection. Although most horses can benefit in some way from being ridden like this, this approach is particularly good for those with a weak back, those with a naturally high head carriage, and horses who are resistant to a contact or don't go forwards when you try to collect them.

'CLOSING THE EXIT ROUTES'

Rather than *doing* things to get the horse into self-carriage, it can be useful to look at what 'exit routes' the horse is taking to avoid working really well. What I mean by 'exit routes' are the various ways his energy will seep out or escape, rather than being gathered together and channelled into collection. As you close the exit routes, the horse will work better and come on the bit without you having to be so proactive.

I really want the sense that the horse and I are working together, which means the horse goes on the bit or finds a nice carriage himself, so I can enjoy the ride without having to force him or work hard myself. One of the main ways to achieve this – apart from sitting as balanced as possible in the saddle – is to notice where his energies are escaping, and then close those exit routes.

EXAMPLES OF SOME COMMON EXIT ROUTES

• The horse is leaning on one shoulder.
SOLUTION: Support him more with the rein on the same side that his shoulder is escaping. Also straighten his head a little.

• The horse is pushing forwards through the bridle (picture 1).
SOLUTION: Ride circles, turns and transitions, and if necessary, go back to the exercises described in 'Soft Mouth', page 80.

• The horse bends his head too much to one side.
SOLUTION: Ask him to straighten his head with your rein and/or leg (picture 2).

Arnie is a big strong horse, which is why I endeavour to avoid any arguments where his strength might win! But here is an example of him pushing through the bridle, rather than softening into a nice carriage. This is a very common exit route for horses, to avoid really collecting themselves. I probably need to try something different here, such as asking for more softness in walk or trot before cantering, and perhaps asking for a little more flexion to the inside with his head, or riding some circles and turns. I could also be softer in my back and legs, to help him 'let go'.

Because the horse's head is turned too much to the inside, he is falling out through his outside shoulder, and leaning his weight upon it. If his head and neck were a little straighter, he would be more likely to carry himself on his inside hind leg instead.

• The horse is slowing down/not really going forwards from his hindquarters (picture 3).
SOLUTION: Create more 'go', tune him up to the leg and stick, ride outdoors, or try opening the front door a little by relaxing the reins and allowing him to really go.

• The horse is slipping out sideways through the ribs.
SOLUTION: Teach him to yield from the ground. Make sure he isn't feeling squashed between hand and leg. Ride circles in different directions, asking him to bend well. Lateral movements such as shoulder-in will really help.

• He is carrying his haunches to one side.
SOLUTION: With both reins, ask his forehand to move across until it is in front of his haunches. Ride shoulder-in to help him place his haunches easily on both sides, as a result of which he will be better able to go straight.

✓ DOs
• Sit softly with your full seat on the saddle.
• Use suppling and gymnastic exercises with the horse that 'do the work for you'.
• Look carefully at how the horse is avoiding collecting by escaping through any of the 'exit routes' described on these pages.

✗ DON'Ts
• Don't be in a hurry.
• Don't get strong with your hands, legs or back.
• Don't sit down hard or stiffly in the saddle.
• Don't just pull the horse's head in.

Suggested exercises to improve the horse's carriage

• Lots of transitions
• Lateral movements such as shoulder-in and half-pass
• Small circles, squares and spirals
• Riding up and down hills

Fantastique is not really going forwards from her hindquarters here, so she is a little hollow in her back and is not relaxed in her poll and jaw: you can see how she is mirroring me because I too look 'braced'. The solution would be for me to soften myself and to ask her to step up a little more from behind, so she can reach forwards into the bridle and find better carriage.

Courageous, Trustworthy and Sensible

It is a fantastic experience to ride a courageous and sensible horse out into the world, knowing you trust one another. Whether you are riding across a wilderness, over a cross-country course, down a busy high street, through a fast-flowing river or into the competition arena, the perfect riding horse quietly asks you if it is all right, then accepts your reassurance and continues calmly and confidently.

As prey animals, it is natural for horses to be suspicious, to react to what they perceive as possible threats to their safety, and to run away from danger. Of course some horses are naturally bolder than others, but a horse with no fear of anything at all is quite unusual and probably not particularly safe to ride!

When a horse begins to trust you, when he follows your leadership and listens to your aids, it becomes possible to take him into many different situations and rely on the partnership you have developed between you… and the more positive experiences you share with him, the more confident he will become.

KEEP HIM LISTENING, THINKING AND STRAIGHT

We have already looked at ways to keep a horse listening to his rider (see 'Listens to the Rider', page 36), but it is only when we take him out into challenging situations that we begin to find out how good our training, leadership and connection with the horse really is.

When you take your horse over, through or past anything challenging, it is important to allow him time to think about what he is doing, rather than pressing him to accept something too quickly. In fact it is a good idea to teach your horse to *stop* and think about it… Have a light rein contact – just enough that you can correct him, sit quietly and focus beyond the object of his fear, looking where you want to go, rather than at the reason why he is afraid to go forwards.

If the horse tries to turn away, quietly use the rein to ask him to be straight, and let him know it is safe. Give him no other options but to stand facing, or to pass the source of his fear, and wait for him to continue going forwards. You may be able to push a horse past something fearful, but it is usually better to give him the time he needs to go past it: that way he gains more confidence from the experience and will trust you more on the next occasion you say something is safe to pass.

The quiet use of one rein or the other, a hand gently patting his neck or a reassuring voice, can help remind the horse you are there for him when he is not sure about something.

Perry's Tips

- To help the horse go past something he is unsure about, a good tip is to turn his head slightly away from the source of his apprehension; this also makes it harder for him to run away through the shoulder, whereas if his head is turned towards the source of his fear, he is more able to run away from it.

- Helping a horse to become courageous, trustworthy and sensible in any situation is a progressive job that takes time. If you progress in small steps, this part of his training can be a source of fun and challenge for both you and the horse, and a great way to really get to know each other.

- As much as possible, it is important to begin each new challenge in a safe and familiar environment – for example an arena or home territory – rather than over-facing the horse with something that scares him more than he, or you, can handle.

SMALL BEGINNINGS

A courageous, trustworthy and sensible horse is one that listens to you and still performs despite the presence of fear – so we don't want to flood him with fear to the point where he loses his ability to listen and 'stay with us'. That means we must control, as much as is possible, the amount of challenge the horse is presented with: just enough to help him expand his repertoire and increase his confidence, but not too much so that he is unable to cope perfectly well.

Horses are usually less able to stay calm and attentive to us when we take them out of the familiar environment such as the riding arena, but it is the level of obedience to the aids that they have achieved, as well as their training and responsiveness, which will help them do the right thing and find security from being with us when challenges present themselves, wherever we are.

There is a great phrase in the narration of an old video I have, which says something like: 'Never ask anything unwise of the noble horse you wish to ride.' I think that says it all.

One of the most distracting things to come across out riding is loose horses prancing around on the other side of a hedge or fence. Although my horse is excited by the presence of the other horse, she is still trotting pretty straight and being obedient. Notice I am asking her to look just a couple of degrees away from the other horse with her head.

TRUSTWORTHY WITH FLAPPING OBJECTS

Many horses are afraid of flapping objects such as plastic bags, so it is a good idea to teach the horse to be trustworthy with such items.

To teach the horse to be non-reactive to flapping sights and sounds, begin somewhere familiar such as the arena; use a very small rustling bag, so the horse doesn't react to it. You may need to screw the bag up so small that it is all but hidden in your hand to begin with.

Stand with a passive body posture whilst stroking the horse's neck or shoulder with your hand, and then do the same thing with the bag (picture 1). As he relaxes, increase the challenge by making the bag gradually bigger and/or stroking him in more delicate areas such as on his head (picture 2).

If he reacts by moving away from the bag, calmly follow him and continue *rhythmically* stroking him until the split second he stops reacting, at which point you should STOP stroking him. This makes him realize that non-reaction is the best option.

Alternatively, make the bag tiny again and return to stroking him in areas that he is quite comfortable with.

Try moving the bag away from the horse and have him follow it (picture 3): this increases his confidence and makes him think the bag is retreating from him. It also triggers his natural inquisitiveness about the bag, so rather than being afraid of it, he may actually become interested in what it is exactly, and in playing with it.

Horses love having a job to do, so find ways to make flapping objects a normal part of their everyday life (pictures 4 and 5)!

1) Make the bag as small as you need to at first, so you can stroke the horse without him reacting (you may even need to make it so small it is entirely contained within your fist). Begin stroking him in an area he is comfortable with, perhaps his neck, and take your time.

2) Gradually increase the size of the bag as the horse relaxes. Also go into more sensitive areas of the horse, always making sure he is happy about it, before proceeding further.

3) Try carrying the bag and walking backwards away from the horse so he follows it: this can increase his confidence, and his inquisitiveness, too.

4) Once he is 100 per cent happy with the bag on the ground, you may wish to test yourselves by carrying it when riding... of course you can always let go of it in an instant if you need to!

5) Giving the horse a job to do, such as putting out the trash, is a good way to develop handiness and variety.

COURAGEOUS WITH OTHER ANIMALS

The tricky thing about coming across other animals with your horse is that you can't really control the other animals, and if they come towards the horse, it can trigger his natural response to be afraid and run away. Because of this instinct to flee when something is chasing him, a good course of action is to see if you and your horse can make the other animals move away from you – and when confronted by an on-coming horse, most animals will move out of the way! Of course, if the horse has never seen cattle or sheep before, for example, it may not be a great idea to go charging into a field and try chasing the animals about. Ideally horses are introduced to such sights in the same way that we introduce them to anything: in a gradual and safe manner, so it is possible to cope with any fear reactions that arise and build the horse's confidence slowly.

Noisy dogs are sometimes a problem for horses, but fortunately, most horse yards and horse people seem to have dogs around the place, so it is quite easy to arrange regular exposure to dogs in order to get your horse relaxed around them. Farm animals are not always so easy to find. Horses that live with sheep and cattle are usually fairly good about them, but many horses these days are kept in exclusively equestrian establishments without other grazing animals. If you don't have the option of your horse living with, or adjacent to, other types of livestock, perhaps take him on the lead rope and let him look over a farm gate at the animals, until they become a more familiar sight to him. As with many potentially frightening things for the horse, it may also help to take an older, more worldly wise horse that will set an example to the less experienced horse by not reacting fearfully. As a result of the older horse's non-reaction, the horse learns that a situation – or in this case, livestock – is safe.

Perfect Rider Checklist

Avoid clutching at the reins or grabbing on to the horse with your legs when he reacts fearfully. Sit in a balanced and relaxed way for as much of the time as possible: that way, you are more likely to 'go with him' when he does something unexpected. Look ahead and into the distance when things get 'lively.'

Fantastique and I have just come across these cattle, and although we have actually worked cattle together in the past, it is still making her seem a little on her toes, not least because these animals are young and look quite playful.

TACKLING GATES

Opening and closing gates is not only a useful practical skill for the horse to learn, it is also a great way to get him listening to you and responding to various aids whilst you manoeuvre him around the gate; for example, he will probably have to do a turn on the forehand and a reinback at the very least, much of it while you ride one-handed.

Approach the gate by keeping him straight and giving him time; if necessary, place your stick on whichever side you are most likely to need to support your leg when doing the gate: on the occasion pictured it is my left leg but because Fantastique is experienced and obedient, I haven't needed to change it from my right hand. Wait for him as though you have all the time in the world, and take one step at a time to position yourself at the catch end of the gate. Keep him listening whilst you open and close the gate by being slow, clear and precise. Use your voice if it helps.

Some horses are nervous around gateways and can become agitated and claustrophobic because of the restricted view; this makes them rush the job, or not listen much at all. It is essential to stay very calm and methodical, talking to and reassuring the horse, rather than being brusque or legging him hard up to the gate, which may raise his anxiety or energy levels too much. Horses that rush gates can also hurt your knees or your hands – and I am speaking from bitter experience: my knees and hands have been hurt at gateways, so teach your horse to do gates efficiently so that yours may not be!

When he has done the gate, ask him to stand quietly by the gate latch and reward him with a kind word and by stroking his neck, before specifically asking him to turn away and continue your ride; these are the details that will make him more thoughtful and relaxed at the next gate.

Fantastique is lined up parallel to the gate.

The left leg behind the girth has asked her to yield the hindquarters around.

CONFIDENT JUMPER

The perfect riding horse should be confident and willing to jump reasonable fences, whether his eventual purpose directly involves jumping or not. Training horses to be jumpers is a specialist area and not something we are exploring in this book, but some basic ability and understanding is beneficial for every riding horse.

Jumping can be helpful from a gymnastic point of view because in order to jump, the horse must push off with his hindquarters and arch his back. Jumping is a good way to keep the horse interested, to give him some variety and fun, and also to help him learn to trust both his own abilities and his rider.

Our aim at every stage is to keep the horse calm, conscious and listening to us, so he becomes confident and enjoys himself when approaching jumps that are within his capability, rather than listening to his own fears or worries.

POLES ON THE GROUND

Whether you are introducing a horse to jumping for the first time or retraining a riding horse to be confident jumping, it is a good idea to begin with poles laid on the ground, so he learns to see distances and place his feet. After all, when we eventually ride him over jumps, we want to rely on him to judge his take-off and avoid hitting the jump with his feet. Trotting poles should be laid about four or five feet apart,

and it is a good idea to begin with only one or two poles. If the horse is resistant to riding over them, perhaps because the coloured poles appear strange to his way of seeing, simply lead him over them a couple of times and quite soon he will be relaxed about them, too.

✓ DOs
- Look for fun challenges, but make sure they are safe and achievable, so the horse's trust in you is increased.
- Wait it out (give him time).
- Teach your horse to stop and think.

✗ DON'Ts
- Don't get strong, mad, scared, weak or bullying – these are all signs of the rider's lack of confidence and leadership.
- Don't put the horse into situations he can't handle.
- Don't think the horse is being 'stupid' or playing you up if he is shying – horses are instinctively programmed to be wary.
- If at all possible, don't give up once you've started!

As a preparation for jumping, I like to place a pole on the ground between the jump wings, where the jump will be, so the horse gets used to going between the wings without shying at them.

LUNGEING OR LONG-REINING OVER JUMPS

To build the horse's confidence and to see how well he jumps naturally without the rider, I firstly lunge or long-rein the horse over some jumps.

Before lungeing over the jump, the horse should be well settled in his work on the lunge: it is no good trying to teach him to lunge and go over a jump at the same time. Also, bear in mind that lungeing and jumping are tiring for the horse, so do not keep sending him over the jump time and time again. If he jumps well once or twice on the lunge, I would usually stop doing it and proceed to riding him.

Long-reining is an art in itself and again, if you or the horse are not sure about the actual long-reining, work on that first, before trying to add jumping into the equation.

With lungeing and long-reining, make sure the horse has a reasonable, straight run up to the jump, rather than have him swinging round the corner and suddenly finding himself on top of a jump: we want him to learn to approach the jump and see his stride in the same way that he would when you ride him over it.

For lungeing over jumps, side-reins must not be used. I place an extra pole as a 'runner' up over the top of the jump wing, so the lunge line slides over the jump wing and doesn't catch on anything and frighten the horse.

RIDING OVER JUMPS

Once the horse is keen over poles in walk, trot and canter and he is jumping reliably on the lunge, it is time to ride him over a low jump. It helps to make this jump a cross-pole, because it teaches the horse to aim for the middle (the lowest point) of the jump.

If he is confident jumping the low jump, it is then a matter of gradually increasing the challenges that are set, in terms of height, visual appearance, spread and spacing of the jumps.

Probably the most common reason for horses being unenthusiastic about jumping is that they have been over-faced or had an uncomfortable experience at some point in the past. It is therefore essential that we don't mis-time going into the forward jumping position ourselves, or catch the horse in his mouth as he takes off.

Set your focus very definitely beyond the jump and approach it with the horse as straight as possible. If your horse has learned to see his stride with the pole-work and lungeing, there should be no need for the rider to try and control the take-off: ideally the rider sets things up beforehand, stays out of the way, and leaves the horse to take the jump.

Conclusion

With the help of this book, you should now be enjoying an exciting journey of discovery and many incredible moments with your horse. Creating a riding horse is like an ever-evolving, living sculpture: it takes lots of patience and care, and the ability to give the horse the time he needs to understand and develop. If you have a clear idea of how you want him to be, and work with him as he is every day, with the tools and inspiration contained within these pages, you, your horse and your riding will together reach new levels of partnership, performance and success. And the great thing is, it can continue to grow like that forever.

"At the end of each day spent together with the horse, most of all there is a wonderful sense of satisfaction deep in the soul."

ABOUT THE AUTHOR

Perry Wood is an internationally recognized horseman, and author of numerous equestrian titles, including the widely acclaimed *Real Riding*. He is also the author of *Secrets of the People Whisperer* (lessons in human communication gleaned from his years spent working with his greatest teachers: horses) and is recognized as an expert in communication and coaching – and has regularly featured in the national press and TV.

Perry believes that the classical principle of softness, lightness and understanding are the keys to building successful relationships with horses, and from such relationships, suppleness, collection and incredible results are attainable by anyone.

With his extensive knowledge and extraordinary ability to create breakthrough results with horses and riders of all levels and abilities, he is in constant demand both at home and abroad for his riding and horsemanship clinics.

For further information visit www.perry-wood.com

ACKNOWLEDGEMENTS

A big thank you to...
Jane Trollope and all at David & Charles for 'getting' my vision for this book and working so hard to make it happen.

Bob Atkins for bringing my vision to life through his fantastic photographs, and for being so fun and easy to work with.

Mountain Horse and Equitech for their generous support. Elaine for all her support and for listening to me bounce ideas around, day and night!

Maggie, Emma and Carly for their help.

To all my students at home and around the world for their enthusiasm and for inviting me to assist in their journey with themselves and their horses.

... and of course, to the horses, who are already 'perfect' anyway!

OUT-TAKES

If you enjoyed the pictures in this book, perhaps you will enjoy some of the out-takes too!

Oops

'Is that mud or chocolate?'

It's important to start youngsters in the right way

'We're going where?!'

Don't try this at home, folks!

'Was that really what I asked for?'

INDEX